W9-BMD-335

DISCARD

Also by David Rieff

A Bed for the Night:
Humanitarianism in Crisis

Crimes of War
(with Roy Gutman)

Slaughterhouse:
Bosnia and the Failure of the West

The Exile:
Cuba in the Heart of Miami

Los Angeles:
Capital of the Third World

Going to Miami:
Exiles, Tourists, and Refugees in the New America

Democratic Dreams and Armed Intervention

SIMON & SCHUSTER

NEW YORK • LONDON • TORONTO • SYDNEY

AT THE POINT OF A GUN

DAVID RIEFF

SIMON & SCHUSTER
Rockefeller Center
1230 Avenue of the Americas
New York, NY 10020

For information about special discounts for bulk purchases, please contact Simon & Schuster Special Sales at 1-800-456-6798 or business@simonandschuster.com

Designed by Dana Sloan

Manufactured in the United States of America

10 9 8 7 6 5 4 3 2 1

Library of Congress Cataloging-in-Publication Data

Rieff, David.
At the point of a gun : democratic dreams and armed intervention / David Rieff.
p. cm.
Includes index.
1. War. 2. Humanitarian intervention. 3. Iraq War, 2003. 4. United States—Foreign relations—1989– 5. United States—Military policy. 6. United Nations. I. Title.
JZ6385.R53 2005
327.1'17'0973—dc22 2004059029
ISBN 0-684-80867-6

Essays in this volume originally appeared in the following publications:

"Hope Is Not Enough," *Prospect,* October 2003 www.prospectmagazine.co.uk
"A New Age of Liberal Imperialism?" *World Policy Journal* (vol. 16, no. 2, Summer 1999). Reprinted with permission of *World Policy Journal.*
"An Age of Genocide," *The New Republic,* January 29, 1996. Reprinted by permission of *The New Republic* 1996.
"In Defense of Afro-Pessimism," *World Policy Journal* (vo. 15, no. 4, Winter 1998/99). Reprinted with permission of *World Policy Journal.*
"Lost Kosovo," *The New Republic,* May 31, 1999. Reprinted by permission of *The New Republic* 1999.
"Goodbye, New World Order," *Mother Jones,* July/August 2003.
"The Lives They Lived: Collateral Damage," *The New York Times Magazine,* December 28, 2003.
"End of Empire," *Mother Jones,* June 2004.
"The Way We Live Now: A Notion of War," *The New York Times Magazine,* December 14, 2003.
"Were Sanctions Right?" *The New York Times Magazine,* July 27, 2003.
"Blueprint for a Mess," *The New York Times Magazine,* November 2, 2003.
"The Shiite Surge," *The New York Times Magazine,* February 1, 2004.

This book is for my mother, Susan Sontag.

CONTENTS

Qui veut faire l'ange, fait la bête.
(He who wants to act the angel becomes the beast.)

—PASCAL

AT THE POINT OF A GUN

INTRODUCTION

THE LOGIC OF THE PRESENT MOMENT, WE ARE told by American policymakers across the political spectrum from George W. Bush to John Kerry and from an equally broad range of policy analysts from advocates of "hard" American power such as Robert Kagan to those who extol the uses of soft power and multilateral institutions like the United Nations such as Joseph Nye, is one of American hegemony. Americans are uncomfortable with the term *empire,* and in many ways it does not adequately describe the realities of United States preponderance in the world. Frank advocates of an imperial vocation for the U.S., many of whom, like the historian Niall Ferguson, interestingly are British (will this "Greece to their Rome" never end?), may not have the influence the attention paid to them in the media might suggest. But within the policy elite, there seems to be a broad consensus that, as the military historian Eliot A. Cohen has put it, "in the end, it makes very little difference whether one thinks of the United States as an empire or as something else . . . the real alternatives are U.S. hegemony exercised prudently or foolishly, consistently or fecklessly, safely or dangerously."

Cohen is associated with the neoconservative movement in

the United States, but his view is one that most members of the U.S. policy elite would probably agree with, even while they would certainly differ over the question of, say, whether the Bush administration's use of American power in Iraq can best be described as prudent or foolish. It was President Bill Clinton's secretary of state, Madeleine Albright, after all, who called for an exercise of American power "with allies if possible, alone if necessary." And those who defended the American invasion of Iraq in 2003 against charges that it was illegal under international law were surely right to respond that by that criterion the War in Kosovo in 1999 had been illegal as well.

If UN Secretary General Kofi Annan's assent and that of the UN Security Council had not been a requirement in the Balkans, why was it necessary in the Middle East? There are answers to that, of course, not least the obvious one that the Kosovo war was overwhelmingly supported (Greece being the predictable exception) by the countries of the region whereas the war in Iraq was opposed by virtually every country in the Middle East with the exception of Israel. Nonetheless, the question is a pertinent one and cannot simply be brushed aside, particularly by those who supported intervention in Bosnia and Kosovo and opposed it in Iraq—i.e., by people like me.

Of course, the triumphalist moment in America with regard to Iraq passed quickly. Almost no one, even the staunchest advocates of the overthrow of Saddam Hussein, would still claim that what followed the fall of the Iraqi dictator was the unbridled success they had predicted before the war started. The continued bloodletting on the ground in Iraq, the overwhelming evidence that although U.S. troops may have been welcomed when they toppled the Baathist regime, they soon came to be viewed with hostility by the Iraqi people, who resented the American occupation of their country, and the growing realization, supported even by U.S. State Department statistics showing that there were more terrorist incidents in 2003 than in any previous year, that the world was anything but safer after Operation Iraqi Freedom despite what the Bush administration had promised, might have been expected to shake people's faith in the idea of armed intervention in the name of democracy, human rights, and humanitarian need. But this has not been the case.

The enthusiasm in the U.S. Congress during the summer of 2004 to declare that the ethnic cleansing in the western Sudanese region of Darfur constituted genocide in the legal sense of the term; the demand by candidate John Kerry that President Bush go to the UN and help organize a humanitarian military intervention; the support that these demands received in much of Europe; the offer by both Britain and Australia to commit troops to any "humanitarian" deployment: all of these things testified to the extent to which faith in the idea of imposing human rights or alleviating humanitarian suffering norms at the point of a gun remained a powerful and compelling idea. Despite Iraq, it seemed there were many in both Western Europe and, more importantly, in the United States, where most of any serious troop deployment, if nothing else, at the logistical level, would have to come from, still subscribed to the view of humanitarian intervention enunciated by British Prime Minister Tony Blair in Chicago in 1999, when he argued that "if we can establish and spread the values of liberty, the rule of law, human rights, and an open society then that is in our national interests, too."

It is an argument that the human rights movement had been making for decades. It underscored that movement's campaign for rights in the former Soviet empire and also its campaigns against U.S. collaboration with Third World dictators from Vietnam to El Salvador. When it was taken up during the administration of President Jimmy Carter, who appointed human rights activists like Patricia Derian to positions of authority in Washington, the American right was aghast. Now, as I write in 2004, this language is the boilerplate of the American right. As President Bush's deputy defense secretary, Paul Wolfowitz, by many accounts the ideological architect of the Iraq War, has put it, "if people are set free to run their countries as they see fit, we will be dealing with a world very favorable to American interests."

In the gaps in that sentence—"set free" by whom and under what conditions?—you can hear, in all its pathos, and with a sense of ghastly inevitability, or fatedness, worthy of a Greek tragedy, the Bush administration's profound miscalculation of and wishful thinking about the realities on the ground of postwar Iraq and the limits of what U.S. military power can actually accomplish. And yet arguably, the human rights justification for the decision to invade Iraq stands up to scrutiny far better than the false claims that Saddam Hussein had weapons of mass destruction or the false assurance that overthrowing him would reduce the level of terrorist threat to the United States.

Given the rise of human rights as an over-arching moral context for the exercise of power by Western countries, this probably should not be surprising. By now, the view that, at least where possible, and, ideally, as often as possible, humanitarian or human rights disasters must not be allowed to take place—a view shared by figures with otherwise little if anything in common in their view of the role of international institutions or the authority of international law as Kofi Annan and Paul Wolfowitz—is almost no longer open to question among foreign policy experts. In the United States, only activists on the far left, like Noam Chomsky, on the far right, like Pat Buchanan, and those who belong to the increasingly beleaguered realist school, notably members of President George Herbert Walker Bush's security team like General Brent Scowcroft and General William Odom (whether it was Bosnia, Iraq, or George W. Bush's doctrine of pre-emption, American military officers in the post–Cold War era have been consistently more cautious than their civilian counterparts), have bucked this policy consensus on a consistent basis.

In what may have been an unguarded moment, Robert Kagan, viewed by many as one of the premier theorists for the expansive use of American military power, once said to me that his real position was that the choice America faced was "leaning toward or away from" the use of military force. And the argument of "hard Wilsonians" like Kagan—the phrase is that of another neo-conservative writer, Max Boot—was that whereas the Clinton administration had mistakenly leaned away from using force (often they cited Bosnia and sometimes, though less often, Rwanda as an example), the Bush administration at least had the opposite tendency (neoconservatives have been far less enamored by President Bush than American liberals imagine; Vice President Cheney, and, above all, Paul Wolfowitz, have been their men).

My argument in this book is that in fact the tendency is so widespread that it unites American neoconservatives and human rights activists, humanitarian relief groups and civilian planners in the Pentagon. I lay out the arguments for this claim in the essays that follow. But it would be dishonest of me not to add that I also make this argument because I know myself to have been, at one time, a member of this unlikely assortment of bedfellows. And in the interests of, as the cliché goes, full disclosure, I have included an essay I wrote in defense of this view. It was not the only one I wrote, but this is a selection of my pieces and, in any case, I think it states the interventionist case better than I did anywhere else for, as its title stipulates, "A New Age of Liberal Imperialism."

A writer who deals with war and humanitarian emergency and imagines he or she can be right all the time is certainly deluded and probably either simple or megalomaniacal. I believe I was wrong in supporting the Rwandan Patriotic Front to the extent that I did in 1994 through 1996 in a number of essays that I have not included here. Having arrived in Rwanda toward the end of the genocide in 1994, and seen the graves, and seen that it was the Tutsi-led RPF that put an end to the slaughter, I made allowances and apologies for the RPF's own ruthless conduct that, while not on the same order of magnitude as the genocide within Rwanda, was nonetheless intermittently murderous and barbarous. And it took me years longer to realize that what the Rwandans had visited on the Congo in the name of their own security was one of the great crimes of our time. That they were not the only villains in the Congolese tragedy does nothing to excuse the role they played in a war that took somewhere between one and four million lives between 1996 and 2000 and still takes many lives today, even as officials in Kigali disclaim any responsibility. This sense that having suffered a great wrong makes anything you do permissible is obviously not restricted to the Great Lakes region of Africa. The conduct of the Israeli government toward the Palestinians, though it has not exacted anything like the same toll in lives, is another obvious case in point.

Relief workers talk—it is a humanitarian cliché by now—of the relief to development continuum. In my darker moments, increasingly the rule rather than the exception, I think one would be well-advised to speak of the victim to victimizer continuum. Or is it a Möbius strip? On the evidence of Somalia, Bosnia, Rwanda, Burundi, Kosovo, Tajikistan, Afghanistan, Sierra Leone, and Iraq, it would be hard to prove otherwise. And yet I think the natural human instinct to side with the victims often got in the way of my fully understanding what I was seeing during the now decade and a half I have been at this strange vocation of writing about man-made catastrophes. Certainly, it got in the way of my understanding the real nature of the Kosovo Liberation Army, an error which figures in a piece I have included here.

Those blatant mistakes will be evident and, in some of these pieces, I have included a few afterthoughts. For the rest, I have let the essays and reported pieces stand as they were published, and, self-evidently, unlike the Kosovo and Rwanda pieces, I continue to stand by their conclusions. What I do not stand by, what indeed this book is largely an argument *against,* is my previous conviction that humanitarian military intervention, whether to alleviate massive suffering or rectify grave human rights violations should be the norm that a Tony Blair or, indeed, a Kofi Annan seems to believe it either has already or should become in international relations. This does not mean I always oppose such interventions. To the contrary, it seems to me that consistency, whether of the type practiced by Paul Wolfowitz or Noam Chomsky, is a terrible error when one is talking about wars. It is a utopia, and if my work has any consistency or any merit it is, in my eyes at least, in its fervent anti-utopianism.

For reasons I try to explain in these pieces, or in one of the postscripts to them, I remain convinced that Bosnia was a just cause. And I still wish the United States or one of the European great powers had intervened in Rwanda. But my position is the polar opposite of Kagan's: I believe we should lean away from war, lean as far away as possible without actually falling over into pacifism. Of course there are just wars: the category was hardly retired with the victory of the Allies in World War II. But I would insist that there are not *many* just wars, and that the endless wars of altruism posited by so many human rights activists (no matter what euphemisms like "peacekeeping," "humanitarian intervention," "upholding international law," or the like they may care to use) or the endless wars of liberation (as they see it) proposed by American neoconservatives—Iraq was supposed to be only the first such step—can only lead to disaster.

I did not "need" the Iraq war to teach me this, but my experience of spending more than six months in Iraq in a series of protracted stays while on assignment for the *New York Times Magazine* has hardened me in this view. In a sense, this book is a chronicle of the path I took toward this chastened sense of things that I now have. Iraq, though, was at the center of this journey, and the second half of the book reproduces most of the work I did there. In a previous book on humanitarian action, I tried to make the case that the gap between our moral ambitions and the realities of our world had simply widened too far to be bridged by human rights activism, relief work, or military intervention, and that humanitarian relief groups needed to "opt out" of the role they were being placed in—that of subcontractors to the war efforts of various NATO powers. This is not the direction most humanitarian groups are heading in (the French section of Doctors Without Borders remains a notable though increasingly isolated exception). Indeed, one British humanitarian specialist, Hugo Slim, has written that "there is considerable overlap of moral ends between the Coalition [military forces and civilian administrators], humanitarian, human rights, and development agencies in Iraq and Afghanistan."

Left and right, that is the received wisdom of our day. "The New Military Humanism," Noam Chomsky called it, and for once he was right. My own view is that, after Iraq, this fantasy should have been discredited. Obviously it hasn't. Equally obviously, this book is my attempt to help discredit it, written by someone who was long sorely tempted by what once seemed to me like a way of reducing human suffering but now seems to me like a recipe for a recapitulation in the twenty-first century of the horrors of nineteen-century colonialism, whose moral justification, it should be remembered, was also humanitarianism, human rights, and the rule of law. It is not true that history repeats itself first as tragedy and the second time as farce. It just repeats itself as tragedy, over and over and over again.

—David Rieff
Seattle, July 2004

Part One

THE UN AND INTERNATIONAL RELATIONS LEADING UP TO IRAQ

HOPE IS NOT ENOUGH

The truck bomb that destroyed the UN headquarters in Baghdad on August 19, 2003, has been as shocking to the UN as a political community as the events of September 11, 2001, were to most Americans. Hyperbole? No one who witnessed the outpouring of emotion at UN headquarters in New York or Geneva would think so. But the depth of grief and outrage engendered by the murder of Kofi Annan's special representative Sergio Vieira de Mello, and twenty-one of his UN colleagues, goes beyond the fact that, trite as it may sound, most UN staffers think of themselves as belonging to a sort of extended family. More crucially, they regard themselves as working not just for an institution (as people tend to do at the World Bank or the IMF) but as serving a cause. That cause, as a surprising number of them will say without a trace of irony, is the cause of humanity.

It is easy for an outsider to be cynical about the UN. The end of the cold war had encouraged absurdly high hopes for the organization, hopes that were cruelly deflated by the triple peacekeeping disasters of Somalia (1993), Rwanda (1994) and Bosnia (1992–95). UN peacekeeping had many successes in the past, from Cyprus to Cambodia, and its peacekeeping department won a Nobel prize in 1988. But in Bosnia the moral limits of the peacekeeping ethos were exposed to the world. UN officials refused to accept that they had an obligation to take the Bosnian—that is, the victims' side—against the government in Belgrade and its Bosnian Serb surrogates. They hewed to the most exquisite neutrality, insisting that this is what their Security Council mandate demanded.

For an organization that continued, at the time, to insist that it was morally superior to the governments it served—the bureaucratic arm of the world's transcendental values, as Michael Barnett, an American scholar who worked for the UN on Rwanda, put it—this was an astonishing position to take. Later, too late for the 250,000 who died during the Bosnian conflict, the UN admitted as much. In its self-lacerating report on the Srebrenica massacre of 1995, it concluded that there had been a "pervasive ambivalence within the UN regarding the role of force in the pursuit of peace" and "an institutional ideology of impartiality even when confronted with attempted genocide."

Rwanda in 1994 was worse. Months before the genocide began, Romeo Dallaire, the UN force commander on the ground, warned UN officials in New York—notably Kofi Annan, then head of the peacekeeping department—of the impending slaughter of Rwanda's minority Tutsis by elements of the Hutu-dominated government. Dallaire asked for permission to act against those plotting the slaughter. New York refused, insisting that his job was to assist with the recently signed peace accord, and even reprimanded Dallaire saying that raids against weapons stores "could only be viewed as hostile by the Rwandan government." In fact, the UN, still smarting from a peacekeeping failure in Somalia not of its own making, was more concerned about its own institutional survival than anything else. As Iqbal Riza, Annan's chef de cabinet once he became Secretary-General, put it, "We could not risk another Somalia . . . We did not want the Rwandan peacekeeping mission to collapse." Another UN inquest painted "a picture of a failed response to early warning."

Despite these reports on the Bosnian and Rwandan disasters—which, to his great credit, Annan either commissioned or permitted to be issued after he became Secretary-General—UN officials could (and can still) be found shifting the blame for the world body's often disgraceful conduct on to the member states, and above all on to Britain, France, Russia, China, and the U.S., the permanent, veto-wielding members of the Security Council. In fairness, this is par for the international course. Just as the UN claims success for itself when it mounts effective peacekeeping or nation-building operations (in El Salvador, in Mozambique, in East Timor under de Mello's leadership), while attributing the failures (Bosnia, Rwanda) to the ill-conceived mandates imposed on it by member states, so the great powers routinely blame the UN for their failures, as the U.S. did so infamously when its own bungling led to an unexpected reverse in Somalia.

Still, a culture of blamelessness is so ingrained at the UN that even Kofi Annan—who has probably been more frankly self-critical about the world body's shortcomings than any of his predecessors—could address a passing-out parade of troops from UNPROFOR, the UN's peacekeeping mission in Bosnia, and tell them *after* the Srebrenica massacre, that they had performed admirably. What he meant was that since they had been given an appalling and unworkable mandate by the UN Security Council, they had done the best they could.

The problem here is that UN officials, while insisting, when criticized, that they have no real autonomy, do *not* present themselves as an international bureaucracy, or a servicing secretariat along the lines of the African Union. On the contrary, they routinely make large moral claims for the institution. These claims of moral authority, and the credibility they continue to have around the world, are what makes the UN a central, rather than a subaltern institution. The question is whether these claims should still be taken seriously. That they continue to exert a powerful influence is beyond doubt. If they did not, there would be no urgent discussion of the U.S. needing to turn the Iraq operation over to the world organization to impart some legitimacy to the postwar occupation. But does it really make sense to invest such hopes in the UN? That uncomfortable question is seldom addressed by those who wish the UN well. (Those who wish it harm, notably within the Bush administration, particularly at the department of defense, are another matter.)

In a recent essay in *Foreign Affairs,* Shashi Tharoor made an eloquent case for the U.S. to recommit itself to the principle of multilateralism in international affairs generally and to the UN specifically. (Tharoor, a career UN official and novelist, is part of a talented brain trust around Annan which has also included former *Financial Times* journalist Edward Mortimer and, until recently, American international relations scholar Michael Doyle.) In the course of setting out his argument, Tharoor addressed the issue of the UN both as a stage and as an actor. The stage role is indisputable. The UN is where "states declaim their differences and their convergences." But when he says actor, he means actor in the theatrical sense—someone performing according to a script written by someone else—and not the more commonsense definition of someone capable of acting for himself. "The UN is the actor," he writes "that executes policies made on its stage, sins . . . committed by individual governments are thus routinely blamed on the organisation itself." Using the metaphor coined by an earlier Secretary-General, Dag Hammarskjöld, Tharoor describes the UN as "a *Santa Maria* battling its way through storms and uncharted oceans to a new world, only to find that the people on shore have blamed the storms on the ship." This vision is astonishingly self-regarding. And note the logic of the argument: if the UN can do no wrong, then surely it must be supported, on the "something is better than nothing" principle.

THERE ARE many reasons to support the UN—Tharoor offers some of them in his article, which debunks the quasi-abolitionist arguments of Bush administration officials like Richard Perle and John Bolton—but the fact that it exists is not one of them. The same thing could have been said about the League of Nations in the 1920s or the 1930s. By chance, the *Guardian* recently reprinted an editorial it ran on August 27, 1928, on the occasion of the signing of the Kellogg-Briand pact that was meant to "outlaw" war, in which it made just such a case. "Anyone can point out the weaknesses of the League," the leader writer intoned, "describe its failures, analyse its vices; but the man who does not see that the creation of the League has put man's hope for peace and his nobler ambitions on a new basis is blind to the history of human institutions."

The point here is not to claim that the UN is as great a failure as the League, or to deny its successes, above all in its sometimes heroic efforts to alleviate human misery among the poor—the cause to which de Mello devoted most of his career. The sheer range of issues the UN is concerned with through its agencies—such as the World Health Organization, UNICEF, the UNDP (United Nations Development Programme)—from treaty law to sanitation, and from peace and security to the environment, proves, as Tharoor rightly insists, that it is not irrelevant. The UN's humanitarian agencies are often criticized for inefficiency and corruption, and like any other governmental bureaucracy they have their share of fools and knaves. But these specialized UN agencies remain the court of last resort for refugees, child soldiers, and, indeed, for the billions of people in the poor world, above all the hundreds of millions in sub-Saharan Africa.

Still, the UN was not founded as some giant alleviation machine—the International Committee of the Red Cross writ large—even though human rights, justice, better living standards, and human dignity are mentioned in the UN charter. It was founded first and foremost as a peace and security institution, designed, as the charter put it, to "save succeeding generations from the scourge of war" and to "maintain international peace and security." UN officials now routinely claim that peace and security are only one imperative among several. But this is historically inaccurate and self-serving. The UN was founded as a central part of the postwar answer to Nazism. It was not created to bring relief, valuable as such a mission is. Indeed, if the failures of UN peacekeeping in the 1990s really are the pattern of the world organization's future, if the UN is incapable of autonomous action in the field of peace and security, and if all it can now be is a giant diplomatic talking shop and a giant relief and development institution, then the case for abolition is far stronger than even the UN's critics have previously suggested.

This may not be the case. Certainly, the war in Iraq has demonstrated the limits of American unilateralism as clearly as it has demonstrated the reality of the U.S.'s unprecedented military power. And "cleaning up" after U.S. invasions of the new type—Kosovo, Afghanistan, Iraq—may indeed afford the UN a role as a de facto colonial office to U.S. power. It is still, however, unclear whether the UN will either accept or be invited to play such a role. What is clear is that being fuelled with good intentions is not enough. If the UN is worth defending, it must be because of what it accomplishes, not for some radiant future it may lead us to. After Communism, we should be inoculated permanently against radiant futures. And the example of the League of Nations should serve as a cautionary tale for those who wish to think seriously, rather than sentimentally, about the UN.

Proponents of the UN often remark that if the world body did not exist, it would have to be invented again. Doubtless this is true. The need for what we now call multilateral solutions to international problems did not begin with the founding of the UN in 1945, nor will it end when it is eventually superseded, as it will be one day. But the UN is an institution with a particular history and a specific set of underlying assumptions. It is an intergovernmental institution; in other words, a body comprising—and with a secretariat responsible to—the world's *states,* not the world's *peoples.* Notwithstanding Annan's attempts to challenge an unqualified reading of sovereignty—in which states are free to do anything within their own borders—the UN's bedrock assumption remains state sovereignty. This is what has made going beyond the rhetorical commitment to human rights—a hallmark of Annan's tenure—so fraught. And it is perhaps why the UN can never live up to the expectations of the world's peoples, even though for some it continues to incarnate them.

For all its pretensions to moral leadership, the UN remains the product of the postwar period in which it was established. Its charter emerged from the negotiations between the founding members in 1944 and 1945, as Stephen Schlesinger details in a fascinating book, *Act of Creation.* And it is only sensible to imagine that another global body might well be configured differently and be better equipped to cope with a world that has changed out of all recognition. To say that an institution has outlived its time is not the same thing as saying it is useless. The UN presided with great intelligence and commitment over the dissolution of Europe's colonial empires (the last mission of this type was de Mello's UN administration in East Timor). But the fact that it was well-suited to the era of decolonization does not change the fact that it may be ill-suited to the twenty-first century, with its rogue states, WMD, international terror networks, and an interventionist global superpower.

TO CLAIM as William Shawcross did in his book on UN peacekeeping, *Deliver Us from Evil,* that Kofi Annan was "charged with the moral leadership of the world," is to indulge in a preposterous sort of sycophancy that impedes serious thought about the UN's future. Annan has had a long and distinguished career within the UN bureaucracy, which he entered as a young man and in which he has served, with the exception of one brief stint in the government of his native Ghana, for his entire adult life. But he is not the secular equivalent of the Pope or the Dalai Lama: he is a politician, a man of power. The cloying press coverage Annan tends to receive, at least outside the U.S., probably serves to obscure the fact that he is indeed the only secular world leader whose brief is as much concerned with the poor and the powerless throughout the world as with the powerful. A British prime minister or a U.S. president does not wake up prepared to devote most of his day to the problems of refugees in northeastern Congo or pollution in the Strait of Malacca. For Annan, such issues lie at the heart of his work. But as observers of the UN have pointed out since its inception, the world body is not a moral post. Annan is the head of the secretariat of an intergovernmental organization—a body whose charter is virtually silent on the Secretary-General's actual power and role.

Each Secretary-General has defined his position according to his own lights. Dag Hammarskjöld, who held the post between the surprise resignation in 1953 of Trygve Lie, the first Secretary-General, and his own mysterious 1961 death in Congo, was probably the most daring. The much underrated U Thant, who succeeded Hammarskjöld and served until 1971, took many more risks than he is usually given credit for, and went so far as to denounce in public the American war in Vietnam—something it is difficult to imagine either his predecessors or his successors doing. Kurt Waldheim (1972–81) was a Nazi, of course; Pérez de Cuéllar (1982–91) a cautious, canny diplomat; and Boutros Boutros-Ghali (1992–96) so thoroughly tyrannized his staff that when Washington decided to deny him a second term, the rank and file at UN headquarters were hard pressed to come up with convincing expressions of regret. Annan, while Under-Secretary-General for Peacekeeping Operations, impressed the U.S. government by his willingness to cooperate with their (belated) decision to intervene in the Balkans. But while there is much evidence that Annan was an effective official, he gave no sign of any special moral leadership. Indeed, many, myself included, reproached him for not resigning over the peacekeeping debacles in Bosnia and Rwanda, which were under his direct supervision. On form, he seemed a decent, intelligent, refined man, but not someone who would rock the boat.

It is one of the surprises of Annan's tenure, which began in 1997, that this man, who is the first career UN official to become Secretary-General, has been willing to go out on a political limb more frequently than his detractors ever imagined. This is not to say that he has often defied the U.S. On taking office, Annan made it his highest priority to restore relations with Washington and to get the U.S. government to repay the vast arrears in dues it owed the UN. Soon after the attacks of September 11th, the Bush administration defused the dues crisis by handing over $582 million, although the UN claims the U.S. still owes it over $1 billion, mainly for peacekeeping duties. (Total annual UN spending, including agencies and peacekeeping, is over $5 billion.) To be effective, the UN is dependent on U.S. participation and on U.S. financial contributions, something Annan and his advisors recognized from the beginning. His success in patching up relations with the U.S. was an extraordinary diplomatic coup. Annan even managed to charm (or at least neutralize) that diehard reactionary opponent of the UN, Senator Jesse Helms. What it must have cost Annan to make such efforts can only be guessed at. A friend of mine in the Secretariat would only say at the time, "Paris is worth a mass."

The lesson of the League of Nations—from which the U.S. absented itself—played an important role in Annan's calculations. Whatever he may or may not have thought of particular U.S. policies (urging the U.S. to lift Iraqi sanctions in the mid–1990s was one issue on which Annan did challenge Washington, albeit discreetly), Annan remained faithful to his initial analysis of the UN's situation: with the Americans, the world body could succeed in achieving many of its goals, but without the U.S. it would flounder. And Annan's goals were ambitious. In 2000, he convened the so-called Millennium Summit, which was meant not only to chart the course of the UN in the coming decades, but also to set ambitious targets for poverty alleviation, the environment, and education, as well as peace and security. The summit was controversial. Many UN officials privately believed the organization had already hosted too many conferences, and that the gap between the goals set forth and the actual willingness of member states to meet their commitments had grown too great. But Annan persisted; the summit was held—the largest in UN history—and the goals duly set. (The sceptical officials look almost certain to be proved correct, at least in the field of development aid where few rich countries are likely to reach their targets.)

To make even a formal success of securing international approval of the millennium goals, Annan had to secure the assent of the U.S. in a way that his predecessors had never been able to do. The rationale was simple. As Tharoor puts it in his *Foreign Affairs* piece, turning a dismissive metaphor coined by the American neoconservative Charles Krauthammer wittily on its head, "If international institutions serve as ropes that tie Gulliver down, then Gulliver will have every interest in snapping the ropes and breaking free of the constraints imposed on him. If, however, these institutions constitute a vessel sturdy enough for Gulliver to sail, and the Lilliputians cheerfully help him to man the bridge and hoist the mainsail because they want to travel to the same destination, then Gulliver is unlikely to jump ship and try to swim on alone." The image is an unfortunate one—what the delegations from the UN's other 190 member states feel about being called Lilliputians, one can only imagine—but privately both serving and former UN officials make the same point: however much they might grouse about the U.S., Annan would have been grossly irresponsible, both to the UN as an institution and to his role as a political leader trying to further international peace and security, they argue, if he tried to map out a strategy for global governance that did not have the U.S. at its center. Annan's position in this regard is often described as being similar to Tony Blair's. Like Annan, Blair is supposed to think that, for better or worse, for the foreseeable future, the U.S. is the only power that can define the global agenda. If it can be persuaded to act in good causes then those causes will be furthered. But if the U.S. declines to act, little will come of the moral ambitions of the human rights revolution or of the lofty goals set by the UN's Millennium Summit.

There are obvious flaws in this argument. It assumes that the U.S. and the UN, or, for that matter, the U.S. and the British government, really do have the same goals. What if Gulliver wants to sail one way and the Lilliputians another? Or what if the Lilliputians, small though they may be, don't want to "cheerfully help him man the bridge," particularly if the bridge in question happens to be Iraq? UN officials are at least privately appalled at the demands made by many U.S. political figures and commentators that America be given special privileges at the UN. This stance is exemplified by Washington's annual demand in the Security Council—so far grudgingly granted—for exemption for its personnel from the rules of the new International Criminal Court. But might cannot make right, protest the critics of the UN's "Gulliver strategy," holding up Iraq as evidence for their conviction that in its desperation not to alienate the U.S., the UN is becoming too compliant. They point out that, despite the fact that most

UN member states opposed the war and Annan himself spoke out repeatedly against it, as soon as the war ended, the Secretariat was more than willing to help the U.S. pass a security council resolution recognizing the postwar occupation by U.S. and British forces and authorizing the UN to send a special representative to Iraq.

That special representative was, of course, Sergio Vieira de Mello. For many reasons, de Mello did not want to take up the post. He had only recently been appointed UN High Commissioner for Human Rights. An ambitious and self-confident man, of formidable intellectual gifts, courage and charisma, he was widely touted as a future Secretary General. And he had never refused an assignment, above all from Kofi Annan, an old friend. He had left the UNHCR to be the UN's proconsul in Sarajevo in 1994. He had left the post of head of the UN Office for the Coordination of Humanitarian Affairs (OCHA) briefly to run the UN authority in Kosovo after the Serbs withdrew, and, later, to become the transitional administrator of newly freed East Timor. But he had not wanted to go to Baghdad, and only agreed to serve for a four-month, nonrenewable period—a term that had less than six weeks to run when he was murdered. Before he went to Baghdad, he complained that he had virtually no authority, an unclear mandate, and that the chances of the UN being made the scapegoat for any failures on the part of the U.S. occupation authorities were high. Once he got there, he went to work with a will, almost single-handedly making it possible for the U.S. administrator, L. Paul Bremer III, to set up the Iraqi Governing Council. But he never liked the mission. "Pray for me," he told a journalist friend shortly before his assassination.

De Mello's predicament was exactly the one that critics of the

UN's "keep the U.S. on board at any cost" had feared. Perhaps Annan had feared it as well. After de Mello's death, Annan said publicly that any future UN role would require a much clearer and more elaborated mandate. And yet it seemed safe to assume that within a fairly short period of time, the Secretary-General would push the UN back towards the role it had played throughout his tenure—that of good soldier. UN officials were painfully aware that they would do a better job in postwar Iraq than the Americans were doing. Postconflict reconstruction and governance was, after all, as much the UN's forte as war was the U.S.'s forte. So there were ethical as well as institutional pressures to toe the U.S. line, even if this ran the risk of appearing to take on the colonial office mantle. But such an accusation, previously restricted to figures on the extreme left, has acquired a new centrality in the aftermath of the terrorist attack that killed de Mello. The attacks have shown that the terrorists and their supporters inside and outside Iraq make little distinction between the U.S. and the UN. True in Iraq, the UN had long been perceived in a hostile light by many Iraqis because it had directed the sanctions regime. But the fact that Annan, in the name of the UN, had opposed the war (as he had opposed the sanctions), that de Mello in particular had been fervently against it, changed nothing. In the ruins of the Baghdad headquarters, the UN counted the cost of keeping Gulliver on board.

WHAT TO DO about all this once the period of mourning for de Mello had passed? There have been two issues—that of the UN's role in Iraq and, more broadly, of the UN's future. Iraq is the simpler of the two. From the UN Secretariat's perspective, the threat to international peace and security posed by the U.S.'s failure to bring order and stability to Iraq in the first months of the postwar occupation was so grave that a UN role was a necessity. The impediment has been the question of whether the U.S. would be willing to grant the UN enough autonomy to get Security Council authorization for such a mission.

The deeper crisis of the UN as an institution is not subject to the vagaries of political negotiation. Although Iraq and de Mello's assassination brought it into sharp relief, the crisis has been developing for more than a decade. The basis of the UN has always been hope balanced against realpolitik. In the aftermath of the Cold War, hopes were again raised high, only to be dashed first by the failures of UN peacekeeping and more recently by the rebirth of military unilateralism from Kosovo to Iraq.

There are three ways the UN can now go, excluding dissolution. The first is to continue as it is, with all the obvious risks of a slide into irrelevancy; the second is for the UN to become the de facto servant of U.S. foreign policy; and the third is to undertake realistic reform. Suddenly, all those questions about UN reform that were batted back and forth for decades in think tanks and seminar rooms, in studies commissioned by the UN or by sympathetic governments, have acquired a new, despairing urgency. (Should the Security Council expand or contract? Should the number of veto-wielding permanent members expand or contract? How can the military staff committee or the General Assembly be reinvigorated?) Nevertheless, the obstacles that have prevented reform in the past remain—from the narrow self-interest of member states (notably Britain and France's desire to cling on to their vetoes) to the realization that an expansion of the Security Council will make it more discordant rather than less. In these circumstances, serious reform seems unrealistic and realistic reform seems unserious. And it is all made worse by the perception that the U.S., after 9/11, spurns not just the UN but multilateralism in general. To the surprise of his critics, myself included, Annan seems to have grasped the magnitude of the crisis. At a press conference at UN headquarters on September 8, 2003, ostensibly to discuss his report on the implementation of the Millennium Declaration, Annan startled his audience by declaring that "events have shaken the international system. I am not even sure whether the consensus and the vision that the Millennium Declaration expressed are still intact." He said that the UN system as a whole, from the Security Council and the General Assembly to the Economic and Social Council and the Trusteeship Council might need "radical reform" if they were to "regain" their authority. He later insisted that the Security Council needed to be made "more democratic and more representative" with "an expansion in membership."

These statements represented an astonishing departure for Annan, a man who is deeply grounded in the cautious institutional culture of the UN and resolutely optimistic about both the world situation and the future of the UN. It was not that what the Secretary-General was saying was original. In private, most senior UN officials express themselves along these lines at least some of the time. It was his willingness to stop pretending that the UN could sail into the future confident that it was the right institution, organized along the right lines, to meet and cope with the challenges the present already posed and the future held. Whether he will follow through on this is another matter. But Annan is right: it is not clear how to rebuild an international system that is faced simultaneously by the unheard-of challenges of a unipolar world in terms of state power, but also a world in which even the most powerful state is vulnerable to attack by small groups armed with weapons that alter strategic reality. The UN was established in 1945. There is nothing in its founding documents or institutional structures that are relevant to the current crisis. What remains is the hope of a better, fairer world. It is that hope that de Mello died for, and that the UN is based on. The problem is that hope is not enough, as Annan in effect admitted. And perhaps the UN is not enough either, or not the institution through which these challenges can be addressed. That, I suspect, is Annan's real fear. In the meantime, no one seems to have a better idea. A dissolution of the UN followed by the creation of a new world organization less in thrall to member states and less confused about its own role might be preferable, but there is no chance of this occurring. For member states like the UN as it is—powerless by design, in the phrase of writer Michel Feher.

If the UN is incapable of serving as the ultimate arbiter of peace and security in the world, the only alternative is force exercised by powerful member states. But no nation, no matter how good its intentions, has the right, the wisdom, or the capacity to act consistently in the world's interests. To imagine otherwise, as some do in Washington, is even more utopian and ill-judged than the most woolly-headed idealizing of the UN. In any case, as the Anglo-American occupation of Iraq has demonstrated these last few months, and the Israeli occupation of the West Bank has demonstrated these last thirty-five years, force may be necessary but it is never sufficient. The *Santa Maria* seems to have hit an iceberg. Thank God the crew has at least stopped smiling and pretending everything is OK.

POSTCRIPT

I was probably too optimistic about the United Nations' institutional capacity for self-interrogation. For while it is true that the mood within "the house," as UN staffers refer to the world organization, has become increasingly bleak in the aftermath of the Iraq war, the UN's de facto postwar endorsement of the U.S. occupation, and the murder of Sergio Vieira de Mello and his colleagues, and that criticism of Secretary-General Annan, once unheard of, became commonplace by the summer of 2004, the institution's conformist reflexes proved stronger than any current of disillusion, let alone dissidence. Admittedly Annan seized the odd opportunity to go against Washington's wishes, notably in his declaration that the Iraq war had been illegal, in his explicit call to the Security Council in the late spring of 2004, not to extend the annual exemption to U.S. forces serving in UN peacekeeping missions from the reach of the International Criminal Court, and in his implicit criticisms, during the Bangkok summit on AIDS in the summer of 2004, of the Bush administration's policies on the disease. But Annan's appointment of (yet another) eminent-persons commission to "study and report" on the UN's future effectively ended what had been the embryo of a serious debate within the UN about the organization's future.

In the meantime, it was business as usual. Indeed, the Bush administration's "rediscovery" of the UN's utility in postwar Iraq—a revelation that led an administration that, before the beginning of the US invasion, had been categorical in its dismissal of the UN's relevance—was greeted with relief at UN headquarters at Turtle Bay. For Kofi Annan and his team, it seemed, Washington was the prodigal son that would never receive anything but the most cordial welcome home. And on the record, UN officials boasted of how central the mis-

sion of the Secretary-General's representative, Lakdar Brahimi, had been in facilitating the end of the formal U.S. occupation of Iraq and the return of juridical sovereignty to Iraqi control (the gap between the de jure and the de facto was, of course, so obvious and painful that UN officials could do little but maintain a discreet silence on the subject). Off the record, these same officials spoke with rue and bitterness of the way in which Brahimi had actually been marginalized. Like de Mello before him, the Americans used the UN's prestige, then ignored its recommendations. Certainly, no one at the UN claimed that the interim Iraqi prime minister, Iyad Allawi, a former militant Baathist and, subsequently, a British intelligence asset, had been Brahimi's choice. "Bush used Brahimi in his speeches," one senior UN official told me. "We were necessary cosmetically. But once the U.S. decided it had made a mistake with de-Baathification, and it had to get a moderate Baathist like Allawi in power, it didn't matter what Brahimi thought. So we were used like a piece of fancy Kleenex . . . as usual."

Such bitterness was scarcely restricted to those UN officials with watching briefs on Iraq. UN officials who worked in Latin America complained privately that in the aftermath of the UN's climbdown over Iraq, anti–U.S. forces on the continent were reinforced in their suspicions that while there might be a functional difference between Washington and the world organization, there was no ideological difference. "When I go into the field," one UN staffer told me, "my interlocutors tend to simply assume that I work for the Americans. And after Iraq, it's much harder for me to make the case convincingly that I don't."

Of course, the real question was whether Secretary-General Annan really understood the need to make such a case, or the threat to the UN's moral legitimacy that loomed if it truly became impossible to continue to make such a case. Often, it appeared as if Annan's secretariat was intent on being useful to the Americans (and hence keeping them within the UN family) at virtually any cost. Add to this the thunder on the American right with regard to the supposed collusion of the UN Secretariat with Saddam Hussein's regime in the context of the so-called Oil for Food program that accompanied the UN–administered, U.S. and U.K.–inspired sanctions against the Baathist regime between the first and second Gulf Wars, and you had a Secretariat that seemed perpetually on the defensive and almost as perpetually trying to please Washington, or, at least, defuse its ire. In the wake of de Mello's assassination, security was almost the only issue on which Annan seemed immoveable. Everything else, up to and including the naming of a successor for de Mello as UN Special Representative in Iraq, was forthcoming from Annan's offices on the thirty-eighth floor of UN headquarters in New York.

As always, conscientious UN officials pleaded 'force majeure,' and insisted there was nothing else they could do. Perhaps they were (and are) right. But what the Iraq crisis between the U.S. and the UN, and the UN's subsequent climbdown, made undeniable, even to UN true believers, was the extent of the contradiction between the UN's role as bully pulpit for the best of human aspirations and its reality as a subaltern intergovernmental organization more entailed to the hoary nostrum that God is with the big battalions than to the vision of the UN Charter or of the Universal Declaration of Human Rights. Perhaps such "disenchantment" was preferable to the sorts of illusions the UN had engendered among many of the most decent people in the world since its founding in the aftermath of World War II. But then again, while hope is certainly not enough, hopelessness is not enough either.

A NEW AGE OF LIBERAL IMPERIALISM?

PREFACE

This book is, as much as anything, an argument with some of the positions I have taken in the past—perhaps, indeed, some of the positions I am best known for. In the introduction, I try to describe both the extent and the reasons for both the shifts in my thinking and the ways in which my thinking has not changed. The essay that follows is probably the most extreme pro-interventionist argument I have ever put forward. It is also the most sanguine account of U.S. power I ever allowed myself to entertain. As such, after the bitter experience of Iraq—and, however paradoxical it may appear, for me this book is about Iraq even when its ostensible subject is Rwanda, or Kosovo, or the UN, or genocide—"A New Age of Liberal Imperialism" seems very far from me. And yet it obviously would have been intellectually dishonest not *to include it. In the aftermath of Kosovo, and with the catastrophe of Africa in my nostrils and my brain, I could see no other alternative to western military power—above all to U.S. power. It seemed to me that if one was not a utopian (and even the most cursory reader of my work will see plainly enough that if there is anything that distinguishes it, it is its vertebral anti-utopianism; it probably accounts for my lack of sympathy with either the left or its mirror image, neoconservatism), then one could not wait for the world to change: one could only hope to mitigate the horror. The only way to do that, I thought then—and here I cannot claim my views have changed—was with brute force.*

As I say, in the killing fields of a world that I did not then and do not now believe has evolved much beyond the one Thomas Hobbes described, what alternative was there? Here, at least, I agree with conservative writers like Robert Kagan and Robert Cooper who have insisted that the Kantian dreams of perpetual peace so in vogue in social-democratic Europe have little relation to realities outside of Europe. More to the point, they are unlikely to do so in any foreseeable future. The world is governed by force, not solidarity, no matter how much we might wish it otherwise and however much American conservatives like Kagan underestimate the power of solidarity in either its Christian or social-democratic incarnation (give me the latter over the former, but give me either one over neoconservatism!). If I am right, then the alternative seemed to be between sitting by and doing nothing as a Rwandan genocide unfolded, or the Albanian Kosovars were forcibly displaced, or accepting the unpalatable fact that in the world as it is, the only other option was to call for the old imperial powers to do their old imperial thing—that is, however politically incorrect it might be, to wish for the 7th Cavalry to ride to the rescue.

Even today, even after Iraq, I cannot entirely repudiate this view. I do not think consistency is the greatest of virtues, but Emerson's famous remark that it was "the hobgoblin of small minds" always seemed to me to go a bit too far in the other direction. And yet if I think anything today, indeed, if this book argues for *anything, I suppose it is against consistency, against ideology and utopia, and for the proposition that each case must be argued on its merits. In other words, it is an argument against both the interventionist utopia of a Paul Wolfowitz or a Robert Kagan and the anti-interventionist utopia of a Noam Chomsky or an Edward Herman. Where I think I went wrong was precisely in the consistency of the argument of the following essay, which does indeed argue that the deployment of U.S. power is to be preferred to the alternatives on offer. A sounder position, I now think, would have been to say preferable* sometimes. *But my thinking had been coarsened by the catastrophes I had witnessed.*

Such preambles are both necessary and beside the point. To plead in extenuation that my intentions were good quite rightly engenders the retort that the road to Hell really is paved with good intentions. And while that Hell, in my chastened view, is called Iraq, I am not really making any such plea. And so I offer this essay, which probably could serve as a counterargument to the thrust of this book, both in the interests of full disclosure and because even today I am of two minds.

IF ANYTHING SHOULD BE CLEAR FROM THE Kosovo crisis, and, for that matter, from the unhappy experiences that outside intervention forces, whether serving under their own flags, the UN's, or NATO's, have had over the past decade in places like Somalia, Rwanda, and Bosnia, it is that ad hoc responses to state failure and humanitarian catastrophe are rarely, if ever, successful. At the same time, the fact that there is now demonstrably a willingness on the part at least of the NATO countries to intervene militarily in the internal conflicts of other nations represents a radical change in international affairs. The conflict over Kosovo, the first war ever waged by the NATO alliance, was undertaken more in the name of human rights and moral obligation than out of any traditional conception of national interest. Indeed, had strictly practical criteria been applied to Kosovo, NATO as a whole might well have taken the same tack its European members did in Bosnia and attempted to prevent the conflict from spreading rather than trying, however halfheartedly, to reverse Slobodan Milosevic's campaign of murder and mass deportation.

The longer term implications of this further step in the post-Cold War moralization of international politics are not yet clear. Realists, whether they belong to the pure national interest school of a Henry Kissinger or the "lead by moral example" of a George Kennan, are alarmed, as well they should be. For it is now clear that half a century of campaigning by human rights activists has had a profound effect on the conduct of international affairs. The old Westphalian system, in which state sovereignty was held to be well-nigh absolute, is under challenge as never before. As former UN Secretary-General Javier Pérez de Cuéllar put it in 1991, "We are clearly witnessing what is probably an irresistible shift in public attitudes toward the belief that the defense of the oppressed in the name of morality should prevail over frontiers and legal documents."

Whether it is really "irresistible" is of course debatable. Sometimes what appears at first glance as a prescient description of the future can turn out to be little more than an accurate diagnosis of the present. But Pérez de Cuéllar, who, for all his grandee's aloofness, was a far abler diagnostician of his times than he is usually given credit for being, does seem to have discerned an essential shift and discerned it early. The Westphalian system in which he was formed as a diplomat now had challengers, many of whom spoke the language of human rights and derived from this language the belief that, in extreme cases at least, human rights abuses necessitated international intervention. The Franco-Italian legal scholar Mario Bettati and the French humanitarian activist and politician Bernard Kouchner even formulated a doctrine: the right of intervention.

And they and those who took a similar line had a profound effect on the thinking of Western governments. Human rights became an organizing principle for action in the 1990s the way anticommunism had been throughout the Cold War. The result was that most of the interventions of the 1990s, whether they were meant to protect civilians in states that had fallen apart, as in Somalia, or to shield an ethnic group from the murderous intent of its own government, as in Kosovo, were undertaken under the banner of preventing human rights abuses or righting humanitarian wrongs. Kosovo has been only the latest example of this, as President Clinton made clear when he said that NATO had acted to prevent "the slaughter of innocents on its doorstep."

ENDS AND MEANS

HOWEVER, the fact that, while the NATO powers are often willing to intervene, they have also shown themselves almost never willing to take casualties suggests that this commitment is as much about having fallen into a rhetorical trap as about being guided by a new moralizing principle. The means employed simply do not match the high-flown rhetoric about ends. There have been times during the Kosovo crisis, as there were during the Bosnian war and the Rwandan emergency, when it has appeared that Western involvement came about because the leaders of the Western countries no longer found it politically possible to get up at a press conference before a television audience and say in effect, "Sorry about the starving X's or the ethnically cleansed Y's. It's just awful what's happening to them, but frankly they don't have any oil, nor are those that oppress them a threat to us. So you, Mr. and Ms. Voter, will have to continue to watch the slaughter on the evening news until it burns itself out."

Of course, that is precisely what members of the policy elites in Washington, Brussels, Paris, London, or Berlin say in private to one another all the time. But public language, along with public pressure, is often what drives policy. By now, commonplace expressions of realism in international affairs have become, to borrow the Early Christian theological distinction between elite and mass Christianity, an esoteric language restricted by and large to policymakers when they are out of public view. It is the language of human rights and humanitarianism that now stands as the exoteric language of public discourse about such questions. What this demonstrates is the degree to which there really has been a human rights revolution in the attitudes, though not to nearly the same degree in the practices, of the Western public and its poll-addicted, pandering governments.

The fact that it is all but inconceivable that a responsible Western leader could say of the Kosovo conflict what Neville Chamberlain said of Czechoslovakia, that this was "a quarrel in a faraway country between people of whom we know nothing" should be demonstration enough—even though, strictly speaking, this would be no more than a simple statement of fact, all the rhetoric about Albania being in the "heart of Europe" to the contrary notwithstanding. To be sure, a politician or cabinet official will occasionally flout, intentionally or unintentionally, the new moral bilingualism. When, famously, then Secretary of State James Baker said of the breakup of Yugoslavia, "We don't have a dog in that fight," he was breaking the unwritten rule that held that, in public, representatives of the Western democracies were always supposed to insist that they stood ready to defend high moral principles.

But for the most part, what a human rights advocate would probably describe as the triumph of the categorical imperative of human rights—an imperative that, in extreme cases anyway, is held to trump all other political or economic interests or criteria—and what a realist might describe as the hypermoralization of international political action, has taken hold not just as a rhetorical but as an operating principle in all the major Western capitals on issues that concern political crises in poor countries and failing states. The fact that there is, as the human rights pioneer Aryeh Neier has pointed out eloquently, a human rights double standard where powerful countries like China are concerned does not mean nothing has changed.

The problem lies in separating the cosmetic from the fundamental, the makeover from the moral and political sea change. In all likelihood, elements of both figure in. It is not just that the possibility of any senior government official of any Western government speaking as bluntly as Baker did about the former Yugoslavia has receded, at least when the press microphones are on. The changes are deeper than that. The writer Michael Ignatieff is surely correct when he insists that "the military campaign in Kosovo depends for its legitimacy on what fifty years of human rights has done to our moral instincts, weakening the presumption in favor of state sovereignty, strengthening the presumption in favor of intervention when massacre and deportation become state policy."*

By "our," of course, Ignatieff means the Western public that is, as he says, perturbed by distant crimes in a way that it would probably not have been fifty or seventy-five years ago. Obviously, some sectors of public opinion in all Western states have viewed international affairs largely through a moral lens. U.S. relations with China before the Second World War, to cite only one obvious example, were highly influenced by the agenda of the missionaries. What is impressive is the degree to which these largely Christian missionary (and imperial) habits of thought and categories of analysis find their much broader echo in the secular human rights movement of the past thirty years, and how successful that movement has been in persuading governments to act at least publicly as if they shared the same concerns and at least some of the same priorities.

MORAL AMBITIONS

HAD THE consequences of this ascendancy largely been beneficial, and had the actions undertaken by governments in the name of human rights and humanitarian imperatives been as successful as activists initially expected them to be, it would be possible simply to welcome the changed rhetorical and, perhaps, even moral circumstances in which international politics must be conducted. But this is not the case. From Somalia to Rwanda, Cambodia to Haiti, and Congo to Bosnia, the bad news is that the failure rate of these interventions spawned by the categorical imperatives of

* Michael Ignatieff, "Human Rights: The Midlife Crisis," *New York Review of Books,* May 20, 1999.

human rights and humanitarianism in altering the situation on the ground in any enduring way approaches 100 percent. Time and time again, our moral ambitions have been revealed as being far larger than our political, military, or even cognitive means. And there is no easy way out. It is undeniable that the Western television viewer does indeed—and surveys support this contention—see some scene of horror in Central Africa or the Balkans and want something to be done. But "something" is the operative word. Even in situations where the media pays intense attention over a long period of time, there is rarely a consensus that military force should be used, while there is usually a great deal of anxiety about involvement in any operation whose end point is not fixed in advance.

No matter how profoundly the influence of the human rights movement has led to a questioning of the inviolability of state sovereignty, the wish to help and the increasing consensus, at least in elite opinion in most NATO countries, that the West has not just the right but the duty to intervene in certain egregious cases is not matched by any coherent idea of what comes next. This is assuming—and as Kosovo has demonstrated, success is anything but assured—that the intervention has succeeded in bringing the particular horror to an end.

Perhaps this is why, in Western Europe at least, the prestige of humanitarianism increased so dramatically over the past fifteen years. The humanitarian enterprise—giving help to people desperately in need of it—has seemed to cut through the complexities and corruptions of politics and national interest. Here at last, it seemed, was something morally uncomplicated, something altruistic, something above politics. Of course, what the humanitarian movement discovered painfully over the past decade (though many aid workers had understood it much earlier), starting in Bosnia and culminating in the refugee camps of eastern Zaire where aid helped not only people in need but those who had perpetrated the Rwandan genocide, was that there was no transcending politics. Aid undeniably did good things. A vaccinated child is a vaccinated child. But at least in some instances, it also prolonged wars, distorted resource allocations, and, as in Bosnia, where the humanitarian effort became the focus of Western intervention, offered the great powers an alibi for not stopping the genocide of the Muslims. And Somalia demonstrated that what the West saw as a humanitarian intervention might well be understood by the locals as an imperial invasion, which, whatever its intentions, to a certain extent it almost always is.

AN UNSTABLE MIXTURE

AS THE limitations of humanitarianism have increasingly become apparent, human rights has taken center stage in the imaginations of those in the West who continue to believe in human progress. Even many humanitarian aid workers have increasingly come to believe that they, too, must uphold rights, and most of the major private voluntary groups like Doctors Without Borders, Save the Children, or the International Rescue Committee are taking bolder and bolder positions on the need to redress wrongs as well as build latrines, set up clinics, or provide food.

As aid becomes more and more of a business, and private-sector companies expert in construction projects increasingly vie with aid agencies for contracts from principal funders like the U.S. Agency for International Development (USAID) and the European Commission Humanitarian Office (ECHO), some humanitarian workers are coming to believe that the more emphasis they place on human rights (something that private companies are hardly likely to have much taste or aptitude for) the more important a role they will retain. But it is more than a question of corporate self-interest; the way out of the crisis of confidence that humanitarianism has undergone has seemed to lie in the quasi-religious moral absolutism and intellectual self-confidence of the human rights movement.

For Western leaders, these distinctions have very little resonance. The Clinton administration, like its European counterparts, routinely conflates human rights and humanitarian concerns. Kosovo is probably the most extreme example of this, but the pattern has been consistent. The best one can say is that most post–Cold War interventions have been undertaken out of an unstable mixture of human rights and humanitarian concerns. And yet the categorical imperative of upholding human rights and the categorical imperative of getting relief to populations who desperately need it are almost as often in conflict as they are complimentary.

The human rights activist seeks, first and foremost, to halt abuses. Usually, this involves denouncing the states or movements that are violating the laws of war or the rights of their citizens. In contrast, the humanitarian aid worker usually finds that he or she must deal with the abusive government or rampaging militia if the aid is to get through safely and be distributed.

So far at least, there is more confusion than any new synthesis between human rights and humanitarianism. And the consequences of this have been immensely serious, both operationally and in terms of rallying support for interventions like the ones that took place in Rwanda, Somalia, or Bosnia. Somalia, in particular, revealed the difficulty of engaging in an operation that was supposed to end a famine but that ended up as a war between the foreign army deployed to help the humanitarian effort and one of the Somali factions. Americans were appalled to see soldiers killed in such circumstances, and their revulsion cannot be attributed solely, or even fundamentally, either to the pictures of a dead U.S. soldier being dragged naked through the streets of Mogadishu or to the trauma of Vietnam.

Soldiers are expected to die in a war, but the Somali operation was not presented as a war; it was presented as a humanitarian mission. And soldiers are not supposed to die in such circumstances. Even when the U.S. government declared Mohamad Farah Aideed its enemy, and set out to hunt him down through the back alleys of Mogadishu, it did so using the language of police work. Aideed was a criminal, U.S. officials kept saying.

The result was that the American public came to think of the hunt for Aideed, even though they knew it was being carried out by U.S. Army Rangers, not as war but as police work. Casualties in war are understood to be inevitable. Soldiers are not only supposed to be ready to kill, they are supposed to be ready to die. But casualties in police work are a different matter entirely. There, it is only criminals who are supposed to get hurt or, if necessary, killed, not the cops. Again, the fundamental problem has not been some peculiar American aversion to military casualties. Rather, there has been an essential mistake in the way such operations are presented to the public, and, perhaps, even in the way they are conceived of by policymakers. Under the circumstances, it should hardly be surprising that public pressure on Congress and the president to withdraw U.S. troops predictably arises at the first moment an operation can no longer be presented in simple moral terms, or when the casualties or even the costs start to mount.

CONFLATING WAR AND CRIME

THE EMPHASIS, both in Bosnia and Rwanda, on tribunals and apprehending war criminals, however understandable, has only further muddied the moral and political waters. For it cements this conflation of war and crime. One deals with an enemy in war very differently from how one deals with a war criminal. and wars against war crimes, which is how Kosovo was presented at the beginning of Operation Allied Force, must either be waged as the Second World War was waged—that is, until unconditional surrender—or run the risk of seeming utterly pointless when, as in most noncrusading wars, a deal is struck between the belligerents that leaves those who have previously been described as war criminals in power. The tensions of such a policy were apparent at the end of the Bosnian war when Slobodan Milosevic, who had quite correctly been described previously by U.S. officials, at least in private, as the architect of the catastrophe, was seen as the indispensable guarantor of the Dayton Accords.

If the tensions are inevitable, so too is a crime-based outlook about war. Ours is an era when most conflicts are within states, and have for their goal less the defeat of an adversary's forces on the battlefield than either the extermination or expulsion of populations. Actually, there are few wars that do not seem to involve widespread and systematic violations of international humanitarian law, so thinking about war as crime is not just an understandable but in many ways a rational response to objective conditions.

And yet the emphasis on the Yugoslav and Rwandan ad hoc international tribunals, and, more recently, on the International Criminal Court (ICC), has not only created false hopes but false perceptions of what a human rights-based international order implies. The false hopes are easier to categorize. Such tribunals may, like the death penalty, deter the individual in question, breaking, as Michael Ignatieff put it, "'the cycle of impunity' for [certain] particular barbarians," but they cannot hope to seriously deter future criminals or crimes any more than the death penalty deters future murderers—a fact one might have expected the largely anti-death penalty, pro–ICC activists to have confronted more seriously.

But it is by insisting that there is no intellectual or moral problem with demanding that international law should be upheld as strenuously as the domestic laws of democratic states that human rights activists, and the governments that are influenced by them, however intermittently, are engaged in a project that almost certainly seems doomed to failure. Starkly put, its presuppositions do not withstand scrutiny. It is all very well to talk about these laws or courts or imperatives as expressing the will of the "international community." In practice, however, the definition of this "community" is highly if not exclusively legalistic and consists of the states that sign various treaties and conventions and the activist nongovernmental organizations that lobby them to do so.

In finessing this fundamental problem of legitimacy—the ICC, as one of its American defenders once conceded, was largely the concern of "hobbyists and specialists"—and in asserting that a body of law that is the product of a treaty has the same authority as a body of law that is the result of long historical processes that involve parliaments, elections, and popular debate, the activists have in effect constructed a legal system for a political and social system that neither exists nor is likely to exist any time in the foreseeable future. Presented as the product of some new global consensus, it is in fact the legal code of a world government.

NO WORLD GOVERNMENT

BUT THERE is no world government. There is only world trade and national governments. To say this is not to indulge in nostalgia for the Westphalian system or to deny that, in the West anyway, there has been a shift in consciousness toward believing that certain conduct by nations within their borders should not be tolerated whatever the current legal status of state sovereignty may be. Obviously, the power of nation-states to control their destiny is less today than it was half a century ago. And in trade law, there has been a real ceding of sovereignty. Where politics and, above all, in the conduct of international relations that can result in war are concerned, however, the picture is much more mixed. States must wage war, and only the state's inherent legitimacy can make it plausible both for young soldiers to kill and die and for their fellow citizens to support or at least tolerate such a tragedy.

The problem with the human rights approach—and in this, Western governments that have eagerly seized on the rhetoric of human rights are, if anything, far more blameworthy than the activists themselves—is less that it is wrong than that it is unsustainable in the absence of a world government, or, at the very least, of a United Nations system with far more money, autonomy, and power than it is ever likely to be granted by its member states.

A UN mercenary army organized along the lines Sir Brian Urquhart has proposed might well have been able to break the back of the Khmer Rouge in Cambodia or the warlords in Somalia. In places where the interests of the great powers are not involved, the Security Council may at times be willing to grant a mandate for intervention to the Secretary-General. And open-ended UN protectorates in those or similar places, backed up by military force and the mandate to use it, unlike such short-lived operations along the lines of the UN Transitional Authority in Cambodia (UNTAC) that have actually taken place, would theoretically have a chance of restoring the broken societies over which they had taken control.

But even leaving aside the question of whether such a move toward world government would be in humanity's best interest, it is obvious that no such option is now available. Even the prospect, seemingly quite realistic in the late 1980s, that UN peacekeeping would become a central instrument of international peace and security has receded over the course of the 1990s, with peacekeeping reduced to a narrower and more traditional role of post-conflict cease-fire monitoring and truce enforcement. But if the United Nations has been marginalized and if the demands of the emerging human rights consensus among the Western elites have proved to be not just hard to satisfy but hard even to define except in the broadest and most nebulous terms, it is equally clear that the current ad hoc-ism is also unsustainable.

"JUST DO IT"

KOSOVO has seen to that. The conflict there has revealed more than simply the fact that NATO was willing to bomb but not—at least not before it was too late to prevent a second slaughter in the Balkans in a single decade—to take the kind of military action that might have prevented the ethnic cleansing of almost the entire Kosovar population. In Pristina, before the NATO air war began, young Kosovars walked around wearing T-shirts with the Nike logo and their own gloss on the Nike slogan. NATO, it read, JUST DO IT!

In a sense, that is what important constitutencies within the human rights community had been saying as well. Obviously, neither the activists nor the Kosovars themselves imagined the kind of limited, hesitant, politically hamstrung military campaign NATO would undertake when they called for action. And yet this was the predictable, perhaps even the inevitable consequence of not defining that "it." The new language of rights, so prevalent in Western capitals, has been revealed to be at least as misleading about what is and is not possible, what it did and did not commit Western states to, as it is a departure from the old language of state sovereignty.

It is not just that the issues over what the future of a postwar Kosovo would be were fudged from the start. Was the province to be liberated by force? If so, was it to be turned into a NATO or an Organization for Security and Cooperation in Europe (OSCE) protectorate? Or was it to be given its independence? These are only some of the questions that were never answered satisfactorily in Washington or in Brussels before the air campaign began.

More gravely still, there is no evidence that a Marshall Plan for the Balkans, clearly a sine qua non for regional stability even before the bombing started and the mass deportation began, had been worked out. The World Bank was barely consulted; the UN specialized agencies, on whom responsibility for the predictable refugee crisis rests, were caught flat-footed. And most Western governments had to run to their parliaments just to get supplemental appropriations to pay for the war; they had no coherent plan for the future whatsoever. Thus, on the political level, the economic level, and the military level, the West was improvising from the start.

But war, even war undertaken on human rights grounds, is not like jazz singing. Improvisation is fatal—as the Kosovars have learned. Just do it, indeed! A country that ran its central bank this way would soon collapse. And yet it continues to be the implicit assumption of the NATO powers that they can confront the crisis of failed states by making it up as they go along. In Somalia, in Rwanda, and in Congo, the Western powers chose to respond with disaster relief, which both guaranteed that the political crises in those countries would continue and represented a terrible misuse of humanitarian aid. In Bosnia, the emphasis was on containing the crisis. In Algeria and Kurdistan, it has been either to ignore it or exploit it.

FINESSING THE DISASTER

AND YET IN Kosovo (this had almost happened in Bosnia), the West was finally hoist on the petard of its own lip service to the categorical imperative of human rights. It was ashamed not to intervene, but it lacked the will to do so with either vision or coherence. Kosovo is probably a lost cause; it is certainly ruined for a generation, whatever eventual deal is worked out, as Bosnia, whose future is to be a ward of NATO, America, and the European Union, probably for decades, has also been ruined for a generation, Dayton or no Dayton. What remains are the modalities through which this disaster can be finessed, and its consequences mitigated.

It is to be hoped that in the wake of Kosovo, the realization that this kind of geo-strategic frivolity and ad hoc-ism, this resolve to act out of moral paradigms that now command the sympathy but do not yet command the deep allegiance of Western public opinion—at least not to the extent that people are willing to sacrifice in order to see that they are upheld—will no longer do. To say this is not to suggest that there are any obvious alternatives. Even if one accepts more of its premises than I do, the human rights perspective clearly is insufficient.

As for the United Nations, it has been shown to be incapable of playing the dual role of both succoring populations at risk while simultaneously acting like a colonial power and imposing some kind of order and rebuilding civic institutions. The important Third World countries seem to have neither the resources nor the ideological inclination to intervene even in their own regions, as Africa's failure to act in Rwanda in 1994 demonstrated so painfully.

The conclusion is inescapable. At the present time, only the West has both the power and, however intermittently, the readiness to act. And by the West, one really means the United States. Obviously, to say that America could act effectively if it chose to do so as, yes, the world's policeman of last resort, is not the same thing as saying that it should. Those who argue, as George Kennan has done, that we overestimate ourselves when we believe we can right the wrongs of the world, must be listened to seriously. So should the views of principled isolationists. And those on what remains of the left who insist that the result of such a broad licensing of American power will be a further entrenchment of America's hegemony over the rest of the world are also unquestionably correct.

WHAT IS TO BE DONE

BUT THE implications of not doing anything are equally clear. Those who fear American power are—this is absolutely certain—condemning other people to death. Had the U.S. armed forces not set up the air bridge to eastern Zaire in the wake of the Rwandan genocide, hundreds of thousands of people would have perished, rather than the tens of thousands who did die. This does not excuse the Clinton administration for failing to act to stop the genocide militarily; but it is a fact. And analogous situations were found in Bosnia and even, for all its failings, in the operation in Somalia.

What is to be done? The Office of the United Nations High Commissioner for Refugees (UNHCR) cannot solve crises of such magnitude; these days, it is hard-pressed even to alleviate one without logistical help from NATO military forces. The humanitarian movement has even fewer means. In becoming dependent on NATO's logistical support, or, as in Kosovo, in effect serving as a humanitarian subcontractor to one of the belligerents, its intellectual and moral coherence, which is based on impartiality, has been undermined. And human rights activists, for the valuable work they do in exposing brutality and violations of international law, are demanding a regime of intervention whose implications they clearly have failed to think through seriously.

By this, I do not mean the issue of consistency—a debate that, these days is usually framed, "If Kosovo, then why not Sudan?"—although the distorting effect of concentrating exclusively on the south Balkans and channeling what monies exist for aid in its direction cannot but have a devastating effect on Africa in particular. To insist on this point is, when all is said and done, to make the great the enemy of the good. There will be no serious intervention in Sudan; that is no reason for us to turn our collective backs on the Kosovars.

But Kosovo is an anomaly—a crisis at the edge of Europe that comes on the heels of the Bosnian crisis about which the NATO powers have a bad conscience. Even had the NATO countries responded more effectively, Kosovo would not have provided a model for how to do post–Cold War interventions.

A deeper problem is how to replace a chaotic post–Cold War disorder with some kind of order that does what it can to prevent both the worst sorts of repression and ethnic cleansing. A realist would say the effort is not worth it. For those who believe differently, whether it is simply because they find the suffering of people in places like Kosovo or the Great Lakes region of Africa as unconscionable when their countries have the means to set it right, or because they believe that too much disorder, even at the periphery of the rich world, is a clear and present danger, the task is to think through how such an order might be imposed.

A more active, attentive, and consistent diplomacy will certainly be necessary, but so will the occasional use of force. Realistically, this means either NATO or the army of the Russian Federation, or both, since only these military establishments have the logistical capacity to move troops long distances in short periods of time. But it is hard to imagine, after the experience of Kosovo, that there will be much appetite for further improvisation. At the same time, it is evident that America's strategic partners will not be disposed to support a renewed Pax Americana in which the United States acts as the global policeman of last resort, even if America were willing to reassume that role. And it never will, since the American consensus is strongly against such an arrangement.

BACK TO THE FUTURE

WHERE DOES this leave us? One possible solution would be to revisit the mandatory system that was instituted after the Versailles Treaty. Its pitfalls are obvious. In practice, League of Nations mandates became thinly disguised extensions of the old colonial empires, with trusteeships distributed more on strategic than on humanitarian grounds, and neither improved the situation of the peoples of the territories in question nor brought about any great improvement in regional stability. Woodrow Wilson's warning during the negotiations at the Paris Peace Conference that "the world would say that the Great Powers first portioned out the helpless parts of the world and then formed the League of Nations," needs to be borne in mind.

But Wilson's original idea, which was, as he put it, to take temporary control over certain territories in order "to build up in as short a time as possible . . . a political unit that can take charge of its own affairs," may be one way out of the current impasse. The unhappy experience of the United Nations in Cambodia suggests that an ad hoc imposition of a trusteeship is doomed to failure, if for no other reason than supervisory control is simply too diffuse and too subject to political pressure. Had the United Nations stayed in Cambodia for a generation, as, to his credit, then Secretary-General Boutros-Ghali argued that it should, it might indeed have improved that unhappy country's prospects; by staying two years, it provided little more than a short respite. Haiti represents a similar failure to stay the course.

To insist on this point is not to bash the United Nations. The structure of the institution, above all the cross-currents and conflicting interests that find their expression in the work of the Security Council, simply makes it the wrong organization to undertake to administer a new trusteeship system. Regional organizations and great powers are far likelier to be able to devise a system of burden sharing. For all its faults (and the "imperialistic" interests) involved, the Nigerian invasion of Sierra Leone was initially a positive development. The problem was not that the Nigerians came; it was that once there, they had neither the will nor the money to follow up their military conquest with state reconstruction. Perhaps, if General Olusegun Obasanjo really does represent a return to democracy in Nigeria, such efforts will begin.

Obviously, behind the scenes the NATO countries and, above all, the United States would have to exercise some degree of supervisory control over the trusteeships and underwrite efforts at nation building. Funding would be politically controversial (obviously, most would have to come from the Western powers and possibly from the Bretton Woods Institutions) and difficult to appropriate wisely. But, on balance, the costs would still be less than the astronomical figures that will be required to rebuild Kosovo, or, for that matter, were needed to deal with the humanitarian crisis in Central Africa in the mid-1990s. Waste and mismanagement are facts of life. They should not become the impediment to actually dealing with the current disorder and tragedy in so much of the poor world.

It is likely that, were such a system to be put in place, the role of American power might actually diminish over the long term, although in the short run it would probably increase. For the most part, however, except in emergencies, or where the rapid dispatch of troops is required, other, mid-sized nations—rather than NATO powers—could do the actual administrating and the policing. And a structure that would necessarily involve this degree of burden sharing between small, medium, and great powers might also serve useful purposes in other fields of international relations, although it would be foolish to expect too much on that score.

The central point is that a mandatory system could take the insights of the human rights revolution into account without overreaching; it could provide a framework for action that could only be an improvement over the current system—if it can even be called that—in which each crisis comes as a kind of lightning bolt from the blue; and it would not be constrained by the kind of divisions that make any sort of serious action through the UN Security Council all but impossible to imagine.

Is this proposal tantamount to calling for a recolonization of part of the world? Would such a system make the United States even more powerful than it is already? Clearly it is, and clearly it would. But what are the alternatives? Kosovo demonstrates how little stomach the United States has for the kind of military action that its moral ambitions impel it to undertake. And there will be many more Kosovos in the coming decades. With the victory of capitalism nearly absolute, the choice is not between systems but about what kind of capitalist system we are going to have and what kind of world order that system requires. However controversial it may be to say this, our choice at the millennium seems to boil down to imperialism or barbarism. Half-measures of the type we have seen in various humanitarian interventions and in Kosovo represent the worst of both worlds. Better to grasp the nettle and accept that liberal imperialism may be the best we are going to do in these callous and sentimental times.

Indeed, the real task for people who reject both realism and the utopian nihilism of a left that would prefer to see genocide in Bosnia and the mass deportation of the Kosovars rather than strengthen, however marginally, the hegemony of the United States, is to try to humanize this new imperial order—assuming it can come into being—and to curb the excesses that it will doubtless produce. The alternative is not liberation or the triumph of some global consensus of conscience, but, to paraphrase Che Guevara, one, two, three, many Kosovos.

AN AGE OF GENOCIDE

ON APRIL 5, 1994, THE PRESIDENT OF RWANDA, Juvenal Habyarimana, flew to Dar es Salaam in Tanzania to attend a gathering of regional heads of state called to discuss the deteriorating situation in neighboring Burundi. The attention of the meeting soon turned to Habyarimana's failure to implement in his own country the peace accords that were signed, after more than two years of negotiations, in Arusha, another Tanzanian city, in August 1993 and witnessed by most of the leaders who had come to Dar to remonstrate with the Rwandan president. Those agreements were to put an end to the fighting that had raged, with varying degrees of intensity and atrocity, between the members of Habyarimana's Hutu tribe—the overwhelming majority in Rwanda—and a guerilla army, the Rwandan Patriotic Front (RPF), made up of the minority Tutsi, who were now either living in exile in neighboring Uganda and Tanzania, having fled a series of government-inspired pogroms, or had remained at home, where they were deprived of a political voice. This was not a new problem. Antipathy between the Hutus and the Tutsi dated back to the eras of German and then Belgian colonization. Until independence in 1959, the Tutsi had controlled Rwanda (as they continued to control Burundi). For most of the colonial period, the Tutsi had been favored. This preferment was owed to the common practice of European colonizers to rule in part through a privileged tribe—the British through the Ibo in Nigeria, the French through the Kabyle in Algeria—and also to the curious place that the Tutsi had come to occupy, by the early twentieth century, in European "race thinking" about Africa.

In reality, the distinction between Tutsi and Hutu is controversial, and not at all as clear as European explorers and imperial officials chose to imagine. According to the stereotypes, the Tutsi are tall, relatively light-skinned and have aquiline noses, whereas Hutus are short, dark and have broad noses. This perceived rule of appearance pleased European racial theorists keen to construct a theory about the barbarity of all Bantu or "Hamitic" peoples, such as the Hutu, and to contrast them unfavorably with "Nilotic" peoples, such as the Tutsi, who were imagined to be non-African in origin and hence more civilized. The fact that only the Twa, or Pygmy, people, numerically insignificant by 1900, were actually indigenous to the Great Lakes subregion, and that the categories "Tutsi" and "Hutu" were as much social distinctions of caste as they were tribal or racial distinctions, was not taken into account by the Belgian authorities. And yet Hutus and Tutsis spoke the same language (Kinyarwanda), shared the same religious conceptions and lived side by side. What separated them was the fact that the Hutu were largely peasants, whereas Tutsi identity was defined by the ownership of ten or more cattle.

Thus the feudal fantasies of Europe, in which the peasant was the lowest order of humanity, collided with the realities of Central African social organization. For although there were observable physical differences between the Tutsi "type" and the Hutu "type," it was possible, through the accumulation of wealth, for a Hutu to become a Tutsi, just as it was possible for a Tutsi to be ruined, lose his cattle, and become a Hutu. Intermarriage between the two groups, moreover, was commonplace. And since Rwandan society is patrilineal, it was possible for a person to be considered a Tutsi, even if his or her last "pure" male Tutsi ancestor was many generations back, and his or her physical appearance was like that of the Hutu women who had married into the family over the generations.

The views of the colonizers did not lose their authority when the colonizers departed. Quite the contrary. Modern Rwandan nationalism owes a great deal to the Tutsi-Hutu distinction. The Tutsis continued to rule for a brief period after independence, but within months the Hutus seized power. Many Tutsi were slaughtered and many left Rwanda; and the children of those refugees formed the leadership of the RPF, even as the specter of an RPF return provided the organizing principle of the Habyarimana regime and, despite the heroic activities of the small Rwandan human rights movement and some moderate Hutu political leaders, of too much of Rwandan political life. Rwanda, it seemed, would never escape the antinomy between Hutu and Tutsi. And in 1994 this classificatory myth plunged the country into the abyss.

The Arusha Agreement was Rwanda's last hope, but from the start it was frail. The deal included the full panoply of arms agreements, separation-of-forces agreements, and election monitoring agreements that international negotiations usually serve up. It also envisaged the uniting of the Forces Armées Rwandaises (FAR) with the RPF. To police all this, the United Nations Security Council created UNAMIR, the United Nations Assistance Mission for Rwanda, a peacekeeping force that eventually numbered some 2,500 troops commanded by a Canadian general named Romeo Dallaire. Secretary-General Boutros Boutros-Ghali also continued the mandate of his Special Envoy, a Cameroonian diplomat with the improbable name of Jacques-Roger Booh-Booh, and a colleague of Boutros-Ghali's from their days together at the Organization of African Unity (OAU). What the United Nations was supposed to do in Rwanda, in the event that the Arusha accords were not respected by the belligerents, seems never to have been considered by the Secretariat or the Department of Peacekeeping Operations. As with its Bosnian deployment, which by the autumn of 1993, when UNAMIR was established, was well into its second year, the UN seems to have entered the fray unwillingly, but, having received a Security Council mandate, segued straight into its ours-not-to-reason-why attitude of sullen compliance with the wishes of the great powers.

As in Bosnia, where the UN's Department of Peacekeeping Operations obtained a great deal of information about Serb concentration camps and other crimes against humanity that it endeavored to suppress (not to have done so, peacekeeping officials claimed, would have imperiled the UN's mandate to act "impartially" and retain the confidence of all sides), the alarming information that UNAMIR collected was also suppressed by the UN Secretariat. The *Observer* in London recently acquired a copy of a cable sent by General Dallaire in January 1994, less than three months before the massacres began, in which he cites a Hutu informant, a senior Rwandan military official training Hutu supremacist militias, who had been ordered (in the words of the cable) "to register all Tutsis in Kigali. He suspects that it is for their extermination. Example he gave was that in twenty minutes his personnel could kill up to 10,000 Tutsis."

According to General Dallaire, the informant had expected UNAMIR to break up the secret training camps and to confiscate the weapons. But the Department of Peacekeeping Operations refused to authorize such a mission. It would exceed their mandate, senior officials insisted. New York even refused Dallaire's request to protect the UN's Rwandan informer. As a result, Dallaire wrote, "he lost faith in us. He was taking all the risks, and we were not reacting." (The Belgian government, which had an agent on UNAMIR's staff, also refused to protect the informer and also failed to take his information seriously.) Later the UN would absolve itself of blame for the Rwandan tragedy by insisting that, in the aftermath of the American debacle in Somalia, there had been no will in the Security Council to do anything about Rwanda. The truth is that the UN was at least as culpable. Whatever blame may be attached to the permanent members of the Council, it was the UN hierarchy that decided not to bring Dallaire's cable to the Security Council's attention at a time when the genocide was still a plan and not yet a practice.

A part of the explanation lies in the UN's habits of servility, its wish not to raise problems, which the Permanent Five prefer to ignore. In the Rwandan case, the UN's failure was also a consequence of the fact that Booh-Booh seems to have been a singularly incompetent official. But there were ideological considerations, too. In contrast to its position on Bosnia, which was hostile to the government in Sarajevo, the UN found in the Habyarimana dictatorship a member state with which it could sympathize. It was this fellow feeling that informed the astonishingly sanguine reports that Special Envoy Booh-Booh, who had known and been friendly with Habyarimana at the OAU, was sending back to Secretary-General Boo-Boo (as Boutros-Ghali was known among the Secretariat's dissenters). In any case, Boo-Boo was predisposed toward a leader who, like himself, enjoyed French sponsorship, and whose survival in office continued to depend on the goodwill of France.

It is clear that most interested parties outside the UN did not share the Secretariat's optimism. As Gerard Prunier points out in his important book, *The Rwanda Crisis: History of a Genocide,* the Arusha deal was more the product of exhaustion than conviction. It was never implemented with enthusiasm by its signatories, nor was there the degree of international attention that was needed to overcome the lack of commitment of the belligerents themselves. Rwanda had either been at war, or at the edge of war, for most of its thirty-five years of independence; so peace was the least likely of outcomes. As Prunier puts it, the country was "a time bomb waiting to be detonated." And the outlines of the catastrophe were clear to the few who cared to see what was going on. That was why Habyarimana received such a dressing down from his fellow presidents before he boarded his plane for the flight home to Kigali on April 6, 1994.

Habyarimana's plane was a Falcon 50 executive jet that he had received as a gift from François Mitterrand. As long as France continued to support Habyarimana, his hold on power seemed strong. The French involvement in Rwanda, long significant, had been growing deeper as the involvement of Belgium, the former colonial power, waned. France had intervened in Rwanda in 1990 to blunt an offensive from Uganda launched by the RPF, the Rwandan Patriotic Front; and again in 1992, when the talks in Arusha had broken down and it appeared both to the RPF and Habyarimana's governing party, the National Revolutionary Movement for Development, known by its French acronym MRND (later a second "D" was added, in parentheses, which stood for "democracy"), that the political settlement in Rwanda would be achieved by massacre. The RPF was a formidable guerrilla force. Many of its cadres, including its commander, Paul Kagame, had fought with the Ugandan guerrillas in the war against Idi Amin. But the FAR was amply supplied and extensively trained by the French. By force or by negotiation, Paris was determined to prop up the Kigali government.

In itself, of course, Rwanda would have been relatively unimportant to a great power like France. It was small; it had the highest population density of any country in Africa; it had a history of dictatorship and civil strife dating back to independence; and its only tourist attraction, the forest of great apes made famous by the American naturalist Diane Fossey, happened to lie along the confrontation line between government forces and the RPF. Economically, Rwanda was largely dependent on development aid. Its principal export, tea, was not a commodity likely to bring it prosperity. And whatever progress the country did make was wiped out by its rate of population growth. And yet France was interested.

Its interest was strategic. Preserving a French-speaking zone in Africa, the Elysée believed, would, along with a nuclear arsenal, secure France's status as a major power and also secure its permanent seat on the Security Council. After its legionnaires drove the RPF back into Uganda in 1992, however, the French seemed to have realized that a settlement involving some form of power-sharing between the two major tribal groups in the region was inevitable. This represented a considerable shift. In 1991, a proposal had been floated at the United Nations that would have deployed an international peacekeeping force within Uganda to ensure that the RPF abided by its commitment to cease hostilities, but for French taste the plan was too favorable to the RPF and the "Anglophones." But by 1993 it was clear even to the French that, without a settlement, anti-Tutsi pogroms would begin again, while Burundi, which was dominated by the minority Tutsis, would also descend into chaos.

Habyarimana was obliged to negotiate, though he made it clear that his heart was not in reconciliation. The Tutsis of the RPF were not much more accommodating; but the great political shift was taking place within the Hutu community. As Prunier explains in his definitive account of these awful events, the negotiations served to fuel the rise of Hutu extremism within Rwanda. Prunier observes that, by 1992, "everybody was wading in mythology. For the Hutu supremacists of the Habyarimana regime, the RPF was the serpent entering the Garden of Eden where industrious, God-fearing, law-abiding members of the sociological majority were peacefully attending to their bucolic tasks." On the RPF side, "the battle-hardened yet naive veterans of Uganda's revolutionary wars . . . saw themselves as the legions of justice who had come, after years in which their country had been hijacked by evil usurpers, to claim their birthright with the help of all good and decent citizens who were bound to agree with them and rush to their support. If they did not, it was because the government had brainwashed them."

Anyone wishing to untangle these rival mythologies need only read Prunier's extraordinary book. The truth about tribal identity in Rwanda and about the rights and wrongs of the struggle between the government and the RPF was far more complicated than the militants on either side wanted to admit; but, as Prunier notes mournfully, this made little difference. "Myths are so much stronger than the reality they purport to represent," he concludes. And in Rwanda in 1992, "those twin conflictual myths, together, had just started to screw on the fuse of one of the biggest human bombs since the Nazi Holocaust."

The warnings were everywhere. "What are we waiting for?" asked Leon Mugesera, the vice president of a local city branch of Habyarimana's own governing MRND Party. "The fatal mistake we made in 1959 was to let the Tutsis get out. . . . They belong in Ethiopia and we are going to find a shortcut to get there by throwing them into the Nyabarongo River. I must insist on this point. We have to act. Wipe them all out!"

As the negotiations progressed, Mugesera and like-minded Hutu militants began to set up death squads and militias, notably the Interhamwe, the Kinyarwanda term for "those who fight together." They also began to compile lists of the names and the addresses of those who were to be killed. All Tutsis had to be eliminated, but the mass murder that the Hutu militants envisaged also singled out for destruction the Hutu clerics, intellectuals, and village leaders who supported power-sharing with the Tutsi. Even those who shared some of the militants' fantasies about an unbridgeable gap between the two peoples, but remained opposed to the idea that the solution to Rwanda's problems was genocide, were marked for elimination.

Rwanda is noteworthy among African countries for the efficiency of its government bureaucracy. The nation is divided not only into prefectures, but into subprefectures, and even into smaller administrative groupings. From the Belgians, the Rwandan civil service inherited an obsession with lists and records. And that, as we know from a certain European country, where, in the first half of the twentieth century, bureaucracy had also become something of an art, meant that any plan for a final solution to the problem of a hated minority could be carried out far more efficiently and comprehensively than in countries where lists were incomplete and bureaucracies less well-informed about the political views and even of the whereabouts of those it had targeted for death. The enemy lists that Hutu supremacists began to compile in 1991 in prefectural offices in the countryside and ministry buildings in the capital and continually updated and revised until the genocide was launched in April 1994 were no mere rhetorical expressions of racist militancy. They were detailed blueprints for massacres to come.

The Hutu militants began by trying to scupper the Arusha Agreement. In early January 1993 they launched a campaign of murder and arson against Tutsis in the northwest. The reaction of the RPF, which was observing the ceasefire, was fierce. RPF forces struck back, crossing into Rwanda. Unlike their behavior in previous forays, this time the RPF, too, was guilty of atrocities. By the end of February, more than 600,000 Hutu peasants were fleeing the RPF's advance; and half of them were being made refugees for the second time, abandoning camps in which they had settled at the end of the 1991 war. The Kigali government was unable to halt the RPF fighters and again the French intervened. Marcel Debarge, the French minister charged with overseas development, defended the action, claiming that France supported the Arusha agreement and was in Rwanda "only to protect our citizens." Prunier is spendidly caustic about this assertion, as he is generally about France's contemptible role in the Rwandan catastrophe. "The fact," he writes, "that the renewed fighting had been caused by the regime systematically sabotaging the agreement France had supported was obviously not to be discussed. France—and this was an article of faith only questioned by ill-intentioned persons—supported democratization everywhere in Africa."

France fueled the flames, and the Hutu militants seized on the RPF's atrocities to win converts to their anti-Tutsi views—and yet the fighters from Uganda played into the hands of their enemies. Before the February fighting, there had been a considerable body of moderate Hutu opinion prepared to stand up for the Arusha settlement and against the supremacists, but after the RPF's atrocities the middle fell out. In retrospect, Arusha was a pause, not a peace. It was only a matter of time before another crisis enveloped the Lake Countries. Meanwhile, the French continued with their arms shipments to Habyarimana's army, directly and—as a Human Rights Watch report later demonstrated—through third parties such as Egypt, Zaire, and South Africa; and these shipments continued after the mass murder of the Tutsis had begun. For its part, the Museveni government in Uganda was again allowing its former Tutsi fighters to train and to organize, and providing them with weapons and other supplies.

The UN, predictably, continued to cite its powerlessness as a justification for its moral complacence and its operational indolence. There was probably nothing UNAMIR could have done to prevent the distribution of arms to the Hutu militants, as Special Envoy Booh-Booh told Belgian Foreign Minister Willy Claes at a meeting in Kigali in early 1994. Still, given what we now know about the information in UNAMIR's hands, the UN could have used the Secretary-General's bully pulpit to publicize the horrors that had already taken place and to warn of the catastrophe that was about to take place. But that had never been Boutros Boutros-Ghali's idea of his office, and he was already acting with an eye to reelection. The Secretary-General insisted over and over again that he was only "the humble servant of the Security Council," while his advisers hewed to their self-exculpatory conviction that the UN, as one of them told me, "could be no better than its powerful member states wanted it to be." Later a Secretariat dissident would confide privately that, "you have no idea how much the whims and fancies of Pharaoh"—another in-house term of scorn for Boutros-Ghali—"muddled up the Rwanda operation from the beginning."

One has only to contrast Booh-Booh's—and, by extension, the Secretariat's—passivity about the gathering Rwandan storm with the anguished appeals of the non-governmental organizations such as Médecins Sans Frontières, Human Rights Watch and the International Rescue Committee. Even within the United Nations system, there were a few outspoken officials. Michel Moussalli, the delegate of the Office of the United Nations High Commissioner for Refugees (UNHCR) was particularly noteworthy in this regard. He spoke with the forthrightness that has made that organization, in contrast to the UN Secretariat, or its Department of Peacekeeping Operations, so admired throughout the world. If the political deadlock in Rwanda were not broken, he insisted, there would be a bloodbath. No one was listening.

THE BLOODBATH was not long in coming. Habyarimana boarded his plane in Dar es Salaam on April 6, 1994. Along with the three-man French crew and Habyarimana's own aides, the passengers included President Cyprien Ntaryamira of Burundi, who was basically thumbing a ride. It was decided that the plane would go to Kigali first and then proceed on to Bujumbura, the Burundian capital. At 8:30 p.m.—in the spring in the Lake Countries it is still not dark at that hour—the Falcon began its final approach into the Kigali airport, named after Gregoire Kayibanda, the first ruler of post-independence Rwanda, whom President (then General) Habyarimana had overthrown in 1973. As the plane descended, it was hit by two portable surface-to-air missiles fired from a position just outside the airport grounds. The Falcon spun out of control and crashed, by ghoulish coincidence, into the garden of Habyarimana's house, before exploding. Everyone on board was killed.

The genocide began within hours. All over Kigali, and in the days to come all over Rwanda, the Interhamwe began to kill. Over the radio, the call kept going out for the extermination of every Tutsi man, woman, and child in Rwanda, and of the Hutus who opposed this final solution. Roadblocks were set up, manned by young Hutu militiamen. Those identified as Tutsis were killed, as were those Hutus on the enemies' lists that the Interhamwe had distributed. In the villages, people were hunted down. They died by the tens of thousands in their homes, in their fields, and in the churches—Rwanda is the most Catholic country in Africa—in which they had sought refuge. And no matter how many died, the radios kept blaring out the calls for all good Hutus to kill the inyenzi, the "cockroaches," who were polluting the Rwandan nation and preventing it from living in peace.

The killing lasted through April, May, and early June and it did not end, in those areas where any Tutsi remained, until RPF forces under Paul Kagame entered Rwanda and, in a military campaign that is now studied at West Point, seized all but the southwestern part of the country. This genocide was artisanal. It was carried out largely with clubs, machetes, small arms, and cans of gasoline with which people were burned alive in countless church naves and school rooms. Those who were there in the immediate aftermath of the genocide (I visited the scene in late July and early August 1994) had the sense of life stopped in a freeze-frame. There was the mission schoolhouse, the lesson half written out on the blackboard, the notebooks still on the desks. And there were the rotting bodies, lying where they had fallen, while lurking at the edge of the compound were packs of dogs, well-fed dogs. Long after the killing ended, it was literally unbearable to be in Rwanda.

And yet what took place there, much of which was widely seen on the evening news, was widely misunderstood. The old racial fantasies played a role, the sense (Bosnia notwithstanding) that this sort of savagery was a predictable part of the African story. There was the impression that these killings had been committed at close quarters with primitive weapons because advanced weapons were lacking and the people were primitive. This was false. The FAR was well-equipped. If people murdered with machetes, it was because the Hutu leadership had conceived of a genocide that would involve the entire Hutu people. Only by making everyone complicit, through having killed or having a relative who killed, could the "final solution" of the Tutsi problem be made the work of, in effect, the entire Hutu people. This is not to say that we must speak, legally, of the Hutu's collective guilt. But we must speak of their collective responsibility. There is no other way to account for what happened.

The mass flight of Hutus into Tanzania and eastern Zaire in the wake of the RPF victory was an acknowledgment of this collective responsibility. The genocide of the Tutsis in 1994 claimed more lives more quickly than any campaign of mass murder in recorded history; and the flight of the Hutus was correspondingly larger and swifter than any previous movement of refugees. Two hundred and fifty thousand people entered Tanzania in forty-eight hours. Two million people left Rwanda in less than two weeks. The Hutus fled because they were terrified—and they were terrified because 200,000 of them (that is a conservative estimate) had participated in the genocide.

The population of Rwanda before the genocide was about 7.5 million people. The average family size in Rwanda is about ten. That means, at a conservative estimate, that at least one member of most Hutu families had killed. Given the huge proportion of the population that was under ten years of age, it is likely that several adult members of every Hutu family had blood on their hands. To insist on this point is not to diminish the sufferings of the refugees; it is to put those sufferings in moral perspective.

Even for those who saw the Tutsi corpses, the numbers are hard to take in. Still, despite the "Holocaust revisionists" of Rwanda, those who deny that an attempt to exterminate the Rwandan Tutsi took place, or who question the credibility of those who chronicled it, the usual figures given are unlikely to be too high. Long before it retook Kigali, the RPF claimed that a million were killed. Three months later, Charles Petrie, the UN's vice-coordinator of emergency aid in Rwanda, conceded that he did not believe that figure to be "an exaggeration." Philippe Gaillard, the Chief Delegate of the International Committee of the Red Cross, advanced a similar figure before he left Kigali. In November 1994, a new UN report estimated that 500,000 had been slaughtered. That became the conventional wisdom for a time. But Prunier argues that "the least bad" estimate cannot be lower than 800,000 dead, and increasingly, as new mass grave sites continue to be exhumed and Tutsi families return to Rwanda from exile and list the relatives they have lost, the higher estimates seem more and more plausible.

Whatever the actual death toll, it was clear to everyone, at least in its aftermath, that what had taken place in Rwanda had to be regarded as a genocide, even according to the narrowest definition of the term. Hutu radio stations had called upon the militants to kill everyone, even the children, and Hutu supremacist leaders insisted over and over again that the reason there were still troubles in Rwanda was that twenty years earlier the Tutsis had been driven out and only the men killed, whereas the only solution was to kill all the Tutsis. "The grave is only half full," the most rabid of these stations, Radio Mille Collines (Rwanda is known as the country of a thousand hills), kept repeating, "who will help us fill it?"

This time those who did the killing did nothing to conceal their actions. The Turks killed the Armenians in remote areas of Anatolia; the Germans did not situate a single gas chamber on the territory of the Reich proper. That way, people could avoid knowing, if they chose to. The extermination of the Tutsis, however, took place in full view of the television cameras and under the eyes of the UNAMIR force in every city, town, and village in Rwanda. The Hutus claimed, as the Nazis had claimed about the Jews and the Turks had claimed about the Armenians, that the Tutsi were a mortal threat to their survival. There was nothing new in this: the great genocides have always been justified by those who initiate them as somehow preemptive. What was new in Rwanda was that everyone in the world saw what was going on.

And yet UN and Western officials—and officials of a good many African states as well—tried to avoid using the word "genocide" for as long as possible. The reason was simple. The word has entailments. Its use confers obligations. Had it been used while the killing was going on, those countries that had ratified the Genocide Convention of 1948 would have been required to intervene to bring it to an end. No one had a taste for that, not the United States, reeling pathetically from the deaths of eighteen soldiers in Somalia, nor the Russians, the British, or the Chinese. Ten Belgian paratroopers were butchered horribly by Hutu militants on the evening Habyarimana died, and Brussels wanted to evacuate its nationals, not to intervene. As for the French, it was their clients who were doing the killing. They did intervene, at the end of the summer, but "Operation Turquoise," dressed up as a humanitarian act, was in fact a last-ditch effort to prop up the FAR in the southwest, that last area of Rwanda that the Hutu clients of France still controlled.

As for the UN: For all Boutros-Ghali's subsequent hand-wringing, and his reproaches toward an international community that cared about "the rich man's war" in Bosnia but not wars in "orphan nations" like Rwanda, he did not begin to use the term "genocide" until more than a month after the killing began, during a visit to Kigali by the UN High Commissioner for Human Rights. As late as April 29, more than three weeks into the murder, Boutros-Ghali was still insisting that Rwanda was a tragedy in which Tutsi were killing Hutu and Hutu were killing Tutsi. Only a week before, he had sanctioned the visit to the General Assembly of Jerome Bicamumpaka, the militant Hutu leader, to present the Kigali government's "case." And officials of the Department of Peacekeeping Operations insisted, publicly and privately, that, as with the United Nations Protection Force (UNPROFOR) in Bosnia, UNAMIR's mandate required its impartiality. If more "peacekeepers" were dispatched under the same peacekeeping mandate—as was being discussed at the UN and, in fairness, pushed hard by Boutros-Ghali and the peacekeeping officials themselves—these new forces would have to treat Tutsi and Hutu equally. The UN force commander in Bosnia had said that UNPROFOR did not "have enemies, only partners." UNAMIR would act on the same assumptions.

Not that the UN would get the chance to act. In one of the most shameful acts of a government whose foreign policy was replete with shameful acts, the Clinton administration did everything it could to prevent the use of the word "genocide" in international fora with regard to Rwanda. Christine Shelly, a State Department spokeswoman, declared on June 10, two months after the genocide had begun, that "although there have been acts of genocide in Rwanda, all the murders cannot be put into that category." As Prunier remarks bitterly, "If one goes by the State Department's surrealistic reasoning, no intervention should have been made against the Nazi death camps since the German authorities were at the time killing large numbers of non-Jews."

By May, Boutros-Ghali began to be really concerned. Despite American opposition, the Secretariat was trying to organize a new deployment of UNAMIR, this time one that would give the UN troops the authority to enforce a peace rather than to "keep" a peace that did not exist. On May 6, UNAMIR II was authorized, with a strength of 5,500 soldiers. But it was not deployed until three months later. The African countries that were approached by the Department of Peacekeeping Operations made a ceasefire a condition of the deployment of UNAMIR II. This, as the subsequent report of Médecins Sans Frontières made clear, "amounted to giving the perpetrators of a genocide the right of veto over the protection of their victims by the international community." As for the Americans, they insisted, in response to a UN request for armored personnel carriers (APCs) for UNAMIR, that they would only rent them (at exorbitant rates, according to most reports) and that the APCs would have to come from the inventory of obsolete vehicles that the army maintained in storage. And it took more than three weeks for the State Department's Office of Legal Affairs to complete the paperwork.

The effort to organize a new UNAMIR force did not lead to any greater acknowledgment that a genocide had taken place in Rwanda. On May 17, apparently under American pressure, the Security Council resolution on the crisis spoke only of "an exceptional situation" and about "acts of genocide that may have been committed." Such reticence played into the hands of the French government, which was continuing to back the Hutus. Philippe Jehanne, a French intelligence agent, told Prunier on May 19 that "we are busy delivering ammunition to the FAR through Goma." Of course, Jehanne added, "I will deny it if you quote me to the press." And Prunier is not alone in having received such confidences from French officials. The Arms Project of Human Rights Watch, which had followed French arms transfers to Kigali for years, has issued a report that makes similar accusations based on admissions by senior French officials.

When the French finally did intervene in Rwanda, their rhetoric changed. Suddenly, genocide, whose authors they had done so much to prop up, was the central issue. As Prime Minister Edouard Balladur said at the UN on July 13, 1994, "France has sent its soldiers into Rwanda out of a moral duty to act without delay in order to stop the genocide and provide immediate assistance to the threatened populations." At the same time, as Prunier notes grimly, French officials were circulating the notion of a "double genocide," one in which Tutsi and Hutu alike were equally guilty. In this, they were seconded as always by Boutros-Ghali. The distinction between the genocide and the refugee crisis was too much to keep straight. Hutus and Tutsis alike had died in huge numbers: that was all people could take in.

The well-meaning intervention of people such as Tipper Gore only confirmed this confusion. When, to her great credit, she went to the Goma refugee camp in eastern Zaire, she unavoidably gave the impression that the people with whom she was expressing solidarity were part of the same universe of suffering that had begun with the massacres in Kigali in April. In a sense, they were. But in a more important sense, the refugees were suffering and dying in Goma because their husbands, brothers, sons (and sometimes their wives and daughters) had tried to exterminate their Tutsi neighbors. It was a decent and brave gesture of Tipper Gore to help out at an aid station, but it also served inadvertently to distort the reality of what had taken place in Rwanda: the reality of genocide.

THE CONVENTION on the Prevention and Punishment of the Crime of Genocide, originally known as Resolution 260A (III) of the United Nations General Assembly, was passed on December 9, 1948, and came into effect as a binding piece of international law on January 12, 1951. Since 1948, it has been ratified by 120 countries. Its provisions are broad. The definition of genocide obviously includes campaigns to exterminate entire peoples, but the framers of the convention emphasized that genocide was "the intent to destroy, in whole or in part, a national, ethnical, racial, or religious group." The "in part" is crucial, as is the language in the convention that states that a genocide need not be accomplished through mass murder to qualify as genocide. Any of the following acts—"killing members of the group; causing serious bodily or mental harm to members of the group; deliberately inflicting on the group conditions of life calculated to bring about its physical destruction in whole or in part; imposing measures intended to prevent births within the group; forcibly transferring children of the group to another group"—are sufficient to substantiate the claim that a genocide is taking place, and to impose on the convention's signatories an affirmative obligation to intervene to stop it.

The convention asserts that genocide is a crime that has existed "in all periods of history." And yet clearly, like so many of the founding documents of the United Nations, its language is haunted by the memory of Nazism. The founders of the UN, as Dag Hammarsjköld once remarked, created the organization not to bring mankind to heaven, but to save it from hell. And genocide seemed like a paradigmatic instance of the kind of evil that, unlike war itself, the "civilized world" (as the framers of the convention unself-consciously called it) could ban, just as piracy and poison gas had been banned (and mostly stamped out) by previous international edicts. If genocide had always existed, the framers of the convention also seemed to assert, somewhat contradictorily, that it was something new, something modern.

In the linguistic sense, they were right. Until 1944, the word "genocide" did not exist. Toward the end of the Second World War, as the full realization of what had happened in the concentration camps was becoming clear, Winston Churchill had written that the world was being confronted with "a crime that has no name." He was wrong, but only barely. At roughly the same time, Raphael Lemkin, a jurist, Polish-born and Jewish, who was working as an adviser to the United States War Department, had coined the term "genocide," and used it in his book *Axis Rule in Occupied Europe.* "New conceptions," Lemkin wrote, "require new terms." For Lemkin, genocide meant the destruction of a nation or ethnic group—though not, as he would emphasize, its total extermination. In this sense, it was "an old practice in its modern development." To describe it, he invented a neologism, cobbled together from the Greek word *genos* (race or tribe) and the Latin suffix *cide* (to kill).

Lemkin was aware that there were many historical examples of wars of extermination, and in a footnote he adduced examples from the destruction of Carthage to the massacre of the Albigensians. But for him a war of extermination and a genocide were not exactly synonymous. In 1944, he knew about the extermination of the Jews, even if he did not realize the full extent of what the Germans had done—Lemkin estimated that 1,700,000 Jews had been murdered—but he insisted that genocide need not be a master plan for the physical extermination of a people or a group. A genocide could take place even when it was employed partially, as a method of weakening rather than murdering all the members of a people. This kind of genocide, Lemkin thought, was being widely practiced by the German occupiers. In the East, particularly in Poland and Western Russia, it was a way of ensuring that "the German people would be stronger than the subjugated peoples after the war even if the German army is defeated."

Lemkin already understood that the Germans had been waging war "not merely against states and their armies but against peoples." Until Hitler came to power, the evolution of the history of war had been in the opposite direction, largely limited to activities against armies and states. In World War I, the ratio of military to civilian dead was 90:10. In World War II, sixty-seven civilians died for every ten soldiers. And the ratio worldwide is now the exact opposite of what it was at the beginning of the 1914–18 war: ninety civilians for every ten soldiers. The "long period of evolution in civilized society," in which Lemkin discerned a steady aversion to wars of extermination, had been reversed by the Germans. Genocide was thus not only a crime against humanity, it was also a threat to future generations, unless the world committed itself to its prevention.

Lemkin was not a naive One-Worlder. "Many hope that there will be no more wars," he wrote, "but we dare not rely on mere hopes for protection against genocidal practices by ruthless conquerors." And far from believing, as so many people in Europe and America did when the genocide of the Bosnian Muslims began in 1992, that after Hitler there would be no more genocides in Europe, Lemkin saw genocide not only as a problem of the Second World War, but, even more crucially, as a problem of the postwar peace. Genocide, he wrote, "is an especially important problem for Europe, where differentiation in nationhood is so marked that despite the principle of political and territorial self-determination, certain national groups may be obliged to live as minorities within the boundaries of other states. If these groups should not be adequately protected, such lack of protection would result in international disturbances, especially in the form of disorganized emigration of the persecuted, who would look for refuge elsewhere."

After the war, it was Lemkin who almost single-handedly succeeded in bringing about the passage of the Genocide Convention. Today, in the wake of the Bosnian slaughter, anyone wanting to think seriously about the problem of genocide needs to return to Lemkin, to his expansive definition of genocide and his clear-headed realization that it represented not only a moral threat but also a strategic threat. For, fifty years later, Lemkin's worst fears have been realized. By his definition, we seem to have entered what might be called an age of genocide—a period in which the goal of wars will be first and foremost the expulsion or the murder of members of a racial, religious or ethnic group, and their replacement by members of the murdering or expelling group, rather than the military victory of one state over another.

Lemkin allowed himself to hope. He put his faith in the nascent United Nations and in the power of international law. Even before the Second World War, he had been campaigning for a unified international criminal law in which crimes of "barbarity," offenses against individuals because of their membership in a national, religious, or racial group, and "vandalism," the destruction of works of art embodying "the genius" of the other group, would be added to the penal code. And his hope that a genuine international community could be forged out of the experience of World War II was shared by many in 1944 and 1945. If today the United Nations seems like little more than a waste of hope, this should not be held against Lemkin.

In any case, Lemkin's original definition of genocide, as opposed to the way the Genocide Convention has subsequently been understood, and the way Lemkin's intellectual inheritors and popularizers have interpreted his work, is notable for its modesty. Lemkin never claimed that only a crime on the order of the Nazi Holocaust was a genocide. He made no requirement that the genocide be total; nor was he concerned with establishing a quantitative threshold, a number of victims below which the word "genocide" could not be employed. Lemkin emphasized over and over again that the offense against a group could be total or partial. The fate of the Bosnian Muslims would certainly have qualified as genocide under this definition. When Lemkin writes that "even before the war Hitler envisaged genocide as a means of changing the biological interrelations in Europe in Germany," he could as well have been writing about the designs of Slobodan Milosevic and Radovan Karadzic. They, too, did not insist on killing every Bosnian Muslim. To the contrary, the Bosnian Serb campaign of ethnic cleansing and mass murder was conducted most brutally in those areas where there was either a Muslim majority or where the Serb-Muslim population ratio was at near parity. Where Serbs were in the overwhelming majority, Muslims were usually left alone.

For Lemkin, mass killing was only part of what made a whole range of barbaric acts committed by a belligerent in war a genocide. Genocide, he wrote, was "a composite of different acts of persecution or destruction." There were two phases: "one, destruction of the national pattern of the oppressed group; the other, the imposition of the national pattern of the oppressor." Again, a premonition of Bosnia. The Serb campaign of rape against Bosnian Muslim women was an element in such a campaign of destruction; and so, more broadly, was ethnic cleansing. The Serb effort to eradicate the traces of Islam from all the territories their forces controlled, and to replace the mosques with Orthodox churches, as well as the renaming of towns, was typical of Lemkin's second phase.

In the postwar period, Lemkin's definition of genocide was subtly altered. This occurred in part during the negotiations that culminated in the passage of the Genocide Convention. But the change has also been a cultural one. If six million deaths was too exacting a criterion for the ascription of genocide, was any organized campaign of affront against a national, racial, or religious group a genocide? Can there be genocide without violence? Some Americans think so, and since the 1960s the term has been used with increasing sloppiness and tendentiousness, and has been made into a metaphor. Talk of "cultural" and "spiritual" genocide has become a part of the rhetorical landscape, particularly in our carnival of identity politics. As Alain Destexhe, one of the founders of Médecins Sans Frontières (MSF), observes in his remarkable book, genocide has "progressively lost its initial meaning and is becoming dangerously commonplace."

Destexhe is Lemkin's faithful and eloquent disciple. His book is a polemic that calls unabashedly for a return to the most austere and limited definition of genocide. "In order to shock people into paying attention to contemporary situations that reflect varying degrees of violence or injustice by making comparisons with murder on the greatest scale known in this century, genocide has been used in ways synonymous with massacre, oppression, and repression, overlooking the fact that the image it conjures up was an attempt to annihilate the whole Jewish race." His aim, Destexhe insists, "is to restore the specific meaning to a term which has been so much abused that it has become the victim of its own success."

Like many of his colleagues at MSF, Destexhe is still marked by the intellectual influence of May 1968. He worries about the debasement of language and the distortions of a media-saturated culture. And so he insists on strict constructions. In a world in which every crime can be called a genocide—the "hunger holocaust" is one example of verbal inflation that particularly infuriates him—how can there be a serious morality or a serious rationality? Destexhe proposes that the term "genocide" be limited to situations where all counts enumerated in the Genocide

Convention apply, and to no others. "Genocide," he writes, "must be reinstated as the most infamous of crimes, the memory of victims preserved and those responsible identified and brought to justice by the international community."

This anger is tonic and necessary, and it comes from a different intellectual and moral universe than that which informs most writing on genocide. The sentimentality and the lack of grounding in real experience, the weakness for thinking metaphorically about the most concrete of human tragedies, the Jimmy Carter-like need to understand everyone's point of view—all tendencies that are exemplified by the work on genocide of Robert Jay Lifton and others—are wholly absent from Destexhe's discussion. His moralism is based on the need to make distinctions between tragedies. When Auschwitz equals Hiroshima, and Hiroshima equals Dresden, and the crimes of the Waffen SS equal the crimes of the Americans in Vietnam, Destexhe insists, "the real meaning of genocide will continue to be trivialized, and this most antihuman of all crimes will continue to be regarded as one more reason to justify fatalism."

Destexhe's book is the cry of a man in despair, an extraordinary meditation on the nature of human solidarity and individual responsibility in this era of mass murder. Destexhe knows of what he speaks. He is a writer who began as a medical doctor, and he has spent the better part of his life as a humanitarian aid worker. His argument is, above all, an expression of his disenchantment with contemporary humanitarianism (a view that, while less important to mainline American and British aid organizations, has always been central to groups in France and Belgium like Destexhe's own Médecins Sans Frontières).

In 1995, after his experiences in Rwanda and those of

Médecins Sans Frontières (and other groups), which stopped providing aid to the Hutu refugees in eastern Zaire when they concluded that to do so was to serve logistically the authors of the genocide, Destexhe resigned his post. Even had the "humanitarian intervention" in which he participated been less morally compromised by its forced collaboration with the mass murderers who controlled the refugee camps, Destexhe's bitterness would still be considerable. In Rwanda, he writes, confronted with "the first unquestionable genocide since that the of the Jews, the world first reacted with indifference and left the country to its fate until the compassion aroused by the plight of the refugees led to a purely humanitarian intervention." Taking humanitarian action rather than political action, he adds, "is one of the best ways for a developed country to avoid facing up to its responsibilities."

Humanitarianism as an evasion, an expression of political cowardice: this lesson will not be gladly received by many Western readers. But it is one of the central lessons of our savage world. After Rwanda, Destexhe came to believe that the only proper response to genocide is political action. He left the world of humanitarian aid, entered politics, and is now a member of the Belgian Senate. Whether he will accomplish more there remains to be seen; but he is certainly correct in insisting that "human needs cannot be met by humanitarian action alone, although this is generally the only response to world tragedies." In a time when humanitarian operations, along with "preventive diplomacy" have replaced peacekeeping as policy catchphrases, and where the military both in Western Europe and in the United States are spending a great of deal of time preparing for future "humanitarian" operations, Destexhe's skepticism both about their moral and practical utility could not be more valuable.

It is not clear, however, that Destexhe's attempt in his book to define genocide in a manner so restrictive that only three twentieth-century events can be called genocides—the massacre of the Armenians by the Turks in 1915; the Jewish Holocaust between 1939 and 1945; and the extermination of the Rwandan Tutsis in 1994—is intellectually or morally sustainable. Indeed, it could be argued that, if one returns to Lemkin's original definition, Destexhe's claim that there have only been three "genuine" genocides is far too restrictive. It may even be that his definition is, in its own way, almost as much of a misuse of the term as are those wanton uses—"cultural genocide," "hunger holocaust"—that he rightly deplores.

Destexhe does not so much want to return to Lemkin as to the definition of genocide as it was understood in the late 1940s. At that time genocide was commonly understood as a peculiarly modern and Western contribution to the history of barbarism. Of course, the preamble of the Genocide Convention acknowledges that "at all periods of history genocide has inflicted great losses on humanity." But what its framers clearly have in mind is the Holocaust. In the late 1940s, this made sense. And yet, in retrospect, it is not clear that the term "genocide"—as opposed to "Shoah" or "Holocaust," words specific to what happened in Europe between 1941 and 1945 that need never lose their appositeness or their force—could long have retained its moral and conceptual coherence as Hitler's war receded from living memory.

For even as a genocide, Hitler's crime was unique. To eradicate European Jewry, Hitler sacrificed everything else, including the resupply of his forces on the Russian front. There are times in Destexhe's book where he seems on the verge of insisting that there have only been two genocides, of the Jews and of the

Tutsis. Were he to have made that argument, his book would have an intellectual consistency that it does not possess. He wants to insist that genocide is "the most infamous of crimes," but he excludes from his definition not only the Serb campaign against the Bosnian Muslims, but also Stalin's terror famine, Pol Pot's campaign of mass murder and, on a numerically though in no sense culturally smaller scale, the extermination of various Amazonian tribes.

Leave aside for the moment the quantitative question of whether a crime that leaves more people dead than any of the genocides by which Destexhe is haunted can really be considered a lesser evil. Destexhe counts the Armenian tragedy as a genocide. But does it fit his own horrific paradigm? For what the Turks did was not nearly as all-encompassing as what the Nazis did. For a start, the Turkish authorities did not try to kill every Armenian everywhere that Ottoman power held sway. Quite the contrary. The mass extinction of the Armenians of northeastern Anatolia was carefully planned and carried out, and the Turkish authorities wished to eliminate, through murder and mass expulsion (what the Serbs have taught us to call "ethnic cleansing") the Armenian presence in most of the country—and yet the substantial Armenian populations of Smyrna and Constantinople were by and large left alone, and those few Armenians from the northeast who managed to reach the Turkish Aegean were neither hunted nor attacked.

The fact that not all Armenians were killed has been used by Turkish apologists to buttress their obscene denials that a genocide took place. What is most interesting about the Turkish denials is that the Nazi example is often used to support a claim of innocence. Thus the Holocaust may have come not only to define the issue, but also to confuse it. If one principal characteristic of genocide is extermination carried out with absolute single-mindedness, even to the detriment of the genocidal state's other policies and ambitions, and if the other principal characteristic is numerical, then genocide will never really be understood except insofar as it approaches or falls away from the Holocaust. And in this way the Holocaust may be used to exonerate many crimes and many criminals.

Lemkin at least was torn between insisting that genocide was sui generis and proposing that it was one of a series of crimes against humanity that the world community had to declare unacceptable. Destexhe is not so torn, which is why, I think, his argument is not completely sustainable. This is not only because the Armenian genocide does not entirely fit the Nazi paradigm or the Rwandan paradigm, but because there is something morally troubling about the claim that a campaign of mass murder systematically directed against an ethnic group is self-evidently a greater crime than a similar campaign directed against, say, a social class, even if more people from the social class are killed, the campaign goes on longer, and the regime that orchestrates it seems just as much an embodiment of evil. Is it really clear, as Destexhe thinks it is, that the former is guilty of "both the greatest and the gravest crime against humanity" and the latter guilty of a great but lesser crime against humanity?

Is there really so much to choose, such a difference to appreciate, between the mass murderer Hitler and the mass murderer Stalin (and probably the mass murderer Mao, too)? And yet, according to Destexhe's argument, the man who set out to exterminate a social class—the kulaks—did not commit a crime on the moral and legal scale of the man who set out to exterminate a people—the Jews. It is important to be clear that Destexhe is not exonerating, he is classifying. Still, there is something very troubling about a moral and legal classification of depravity according to which Pol Pot's regime in Cambodia, which was responsible for the planned murder of more than a million "class enemies"—one-seventh of the Cambodian population—is less hateful, less urgent in its demand for a response, than the Hutu butchers in Rwanda; in which the fate of the Bosnian Muslims, with which Destexhe sympathizes deeply, is nonetheless consigned to an inferior order of criminality.

It is not clear whether Destexhe is trapped by his understanding of Lemkin's original definition, or is simply at his wit's end in finding a way to combat the indifference that a latitudinarian definition of genocide has engendered in the West. But his passion leads him to misstatements of fact. Destexhe's implicit (and correct) insistence on the radical, unique evil of Hitler's war against the Jews is contradicted by his own characterization of it as "murder on the greatest scale known in this century." If we are discussing scale, then it is important to remember that on purely numerical grounds the famine that Stalin visited on the Ukraine was responsible for more deaths than the death camps and the Einsatzgruppen. Such a comparison may seem a little obscene, but this is really the fault of those, such as Destexhe and the other "strict constructionists" of genocide, who have set up a quantitative standard. Other, unquantitative conceptions of genocide are possible. And they are not so strict that they are useless.

It is unlikely that most of the crimes in which genocidal killing and genocidally motivated campaigns of rape, vandalism, and expulsion take place will be as total as what took place in Nazi-occupied Europe or in Rwanda. Destexhe, like Lemkin, argues that a strict definition of genocide will make people less complacent, more inclined to help bring the perpetrators of the few real genocides to justice. I do not think that he is right. It seems more probable that such an infrequently instantiated notion of ultimacy will make people more complacent, as they dismiss the overwhelming number of crimes that do not correspond to the exacting definition. If I am right, and we are entering a time in which genocide will become more and more commonplace, there will be enough fatalism around without buttressing it with the moral excuse that Cambodia or East Bengal or Bosnia or South Sudan is not Auschwitz or Nyarubuye Mission. In the matter of genocide, strictness of definition can have the same unfortunate effect as sloppiness of definition. Our sense of genocide must be as flexible and as inventive as the human capacity for evil.

Raphael Lemkin coined the word "genocide" as a way of facilitating historical understanding. If the word helps us to come to grips with Rwanda, or Bosnia, or other crimes and tragedies that await us, if it helps us to remember, as Gerard Prunier puts it in the foreword to his book, that "what we have witnessed in Rwanda is a historical product, not a biological fatality or a spontaneous bestial outburst," then let us continue to rely upon it. But the word was always a moral and intellectual shorthand, a necessary but futile attempt to master evil by describing it. If the word itself has become a kind of mystification, a way of forcing the bitterest of human experiences into hierarchies of suffering that no longer make much moral or practical sense, then there is no reason to cling to it. Its referent, anyway, will be with us. The victims will still be there, as will the need for human solidarity, without whose rebirth our world will soon become morally uninhabitable.

POSTSCRIPT

With the crisis in the Darfur region of western Sudan that came to the attention of the Western public in the spring of 2004, the talk of the need to launch a military intervention on humanitarian grounds again came to the fore. Human rights activists insisted that we were witnessing a repetition of the Rwandan crisis of 1994, a cry that was by such disparate groups as neoliberal supporters of the Iraq war like the editors of The New Republic *magazine, the Christian right and its representatives in Congress like Senator Sam Brownback of Kansas, who seemed to oscillate between his concern for the people of Darfur and his advocacy for an amendment to the U.S. Constitution banning gay marriage, and the left-leaning Congressional Black Caucus. At the annual convention of the NAACP in Philadelphia in July 2004, the Democratic candidate, John Kerry, demanded a UN–backed military intervention to stop the genocide. On the other side of the political spectrum, conservative talk show hosts on the radio and on the Fox cable TV channel made much of the fact that France—their favorite bugbear—had opposed the U.S. intervention in Iraq and was now opposing a UN intervention in Darfur.*

Lost in all of this was the question of whether what was actually taking place in Darfur was a genocide. Terms like Arabs killing black Africans might make sense to people who had never been to Sudan, but to those who had the idea that the Arab Sudanese were not *black as well was hard to credit. That there had been massacres committed by the Government of Sudan-supported Jamjaweed militia was beyond question. But again, whether this constituted genocide was not. Indeed, if massacre was now to become proof positive of genocide, legally defined, then basically every intrastate war taking place on earth could be described as genocidal, and this would make the term itself ut-*

terly incoherent. The real question, with regard to Darfur, was one of information and the evaluation of that information. John Kerry, who had not been to Darfur, was convinced a genocide was taking place. Jean-Herve Bradol, the head of the French section of Doctors without Borders, who had been there, was not convinced. Not having been there myself, and, in middle age, increasingly skeptical of any opinion I might entertain about any place where I have not gotten my boots muddy, I am not sure I have the right to an opinion—only to my skepticism, particularly as the rhetoric of humanitarian catastrophe, so familiar from past crises from Somalia to Kosovo, has been deployed and as, with every passing day, the estimates of how many people might *die in Darfur seemed to increase.*

If everything is a genocide, then surely we need another term to encompass Rwanda, the Shoah, the extermination of the Armenians by the Turks. And even if we restrict the term, what is the value of a category that, in law at least, may arguably not include the Cambodian holocaust of the Khmer Rouge, because it did not target a race, a religion, or an ethnic group specifically? That, in fact, was the question posed by "An Age of Genocide."

IN DEFENSE OF AFRO-PESSIMISM

It has been almost forty years since the decolonization of sub-Saharan Africa began in earnest, and more than thirty since the independence of the continent was largely achieved. But what began in such hope—independent Africa will be "a paradise" was the way Kwame Nkrumah, one of the architects of Pan-Africanism and Ghana's first president, put it in 1957, and he was anything but alone in his optimism—had already, by the late 1970s, given way to an ingrained pessimism about Africa's future. This gloom soon became pervasive not only among Africans themselves but among the continent's well-wishers and advocates abroad. By the end of the 1980s, what had come to be called Afro-pessimism dominated the debate. In this view, while Africa's promise remained undeniable—given the energies of its peoples and the vast resources that lay beneath its rich soil, from oil and minerals to 40 percent of the world's potential supply of hydroelectric power, it could hardly have been otherwise—the continent was seen as the one part of the world for which the future was likely to be far worse than the past.

Afro-pessimism was all too amply grounded in Africa's postcolonial realities. The continent's living standards had risen during the first decade after independence but had begun declining in the 1970s, the same period when much of the rest of the poor world—the "South," to use the term of art of development experts and United Nations *conférenciers*—began to make real progress toward sustainable development. In particular, the contrast with East Asia, which, by all the normal indicators of social and economic progress, had been at roughly the same level of development as Africa in the early 1960s, could not have been more pronounced or more ghastly. Between 1960 and 1980, much of East Asia was literally transformed, and some countries, notably Thailand, Malaysia, Singapore, Taiwan, and South Korea, either shrugged off underdevelopment entirely or became, both from an economic and a social of point of view, complicated mixtures of development and underdevelopment.

During the same period, most African countries grew poorer, and most Africans find themselves worse off today than they were at independence. Some indicators, like educational enrollments and life expectancy, have stagnated. Again, the contrast with East Asia, where, for example, average life expectancy rose ten years between 1980 and 1994, could not be more striking. Even food security became an issue in Africa, since the continent's ability to feed itself became more and more of an endemic crisis in many areas by the 1980s. In terms of real incomes, even factoring in the improvements in the economic situation of some parts of the continent in the mid-1990s, the decline is equally acute. And whatever gains in agricultural production have been achieved, they have been more than offset by the vast increase in population, so that less food is available per capita in 1998 than in 1968.

If the agricultural sector is weak and growing weaker, industrial development outside of South Africa, which is a partly developed economy and thus by the standards of the continent anomalous, is all but nonexistent. In macroeconomic terms, Africa's only important role in the world economy remains that of a producer of commodities—principally oil, minerals, and strategic metals. And the fall in the prices of oil, gold, and such commodities as palm oil that began in the 1980s has only further exacerbated the African situation. In fairness, there are statistics that show that in the 1990s foreign investment in Africa is once again increasing. However, when disaggregated in such a way as to show the distribution of real capital flows rather than percentage increases in foreign investment, this seems to represent mostly further investment in the energy and mining sectors and in business ventures in postapartheid South Africa than a massive expansion of international corporate investment in the continent.

ANOTHER "LOST DECADE"

In an era when the volume of world trade has been growing steadily, and in which capital is mobile in a way that arguably it has never been before, it is hardly surprising that some investment flows have been directed toward the continent. However, Africa's overall share of the volume of world trade has been declining, despite what seemed like a sharp uptick in 1995 and 1996. African growth rates have mirrored this trend. The steady growth in real gross domestic product (GDP) in 1995, 1996, and 1997 was impressive, particularly since Africa had virtually negative growth in 1993. But as a result of the Russian and Asian economic crises, the effects of which have churned through the world economy,

Africa's real GDP in 1998 will grow no more than 1 percent. The prospect looms of a return to the catastrophic economic conditions of the 1980s—the period known among economists as Africa's "lost decade."

That Africa would have been severely wounded by a global economic contraction is hardly surprising, since, as even its staunchest supporters have long conceded, what little recovery there has been on the continent remains extremely precarious. There are many reasons for this, but certainly the gravest is that little of substance has been done to ease the crushing burden of the continent's debt. Sub-Saharan Africa owes over $227 billion, $379 for every man, woman, and child on the continent. By itself, the full servicing of this debt amounts to 25 percent of sub-Saharan Africa's total annual export earnings.

All of this has rendered Africa enormously dependent on official development aid and humanitarian assistance, which rose steadily from the 1970s to the early 1990s. By the 1980s, this aid accounted for between 10 and 20 percent of the gross national product (GNP) of many African states. In the 1990s, however, as donors have lost confidence in the efficacy of a development model that has been tried in one form or another since the 1960s in Africa and yet cannot be shown to have substantially improved the situation of ordinary Africans, these aid budgets have steadily been scaled back, both in percentage terms of national budgets of donor countries as well as in percentage terms of GNP of these countries. In the United States, they have fallen to historic lows. And even in donor countries where there is a greater consensus on the need for aid, governments have been increasingly unwilling to disburse funds. There are signs that multilateral aid from such institutions as the World Bank and the International Monetary Fund (IMF) may soon start being cut as well. By most criteria, Africa has received more aid than any other region of the world. And yet, for all the very tangible good it has done, aid has clearly had a far more minimal effect on Africa's development than either donor countries or recipients ever imagined.

WHAT WENT WRONG

THERE ARE probably as many explanations for why things went so wrong in postcolonial Africa as there are commentators. Some have located the root of the problem mainly in the despoliations of the colonial era. Others have blamed the "personalized" state, as it is sometimes known, of the Nkrumahs, Kenyattas, Mobutus, and Senghors, and the kleptocratic habits of the politicians who succeeded them. The artificiality of Africa's borders doubtless played a role in impeding political development. Alongside all these explanations, there is the colder fact that Africa entered the world economy at a moment when neither the cheap labor nor mineral riches that were really all it could bring to the economic table sufficed—given the corruption of most African regimes—to lead it to sustainable economic development. Some development officials and African intellectuals, while acknowledging this, claim that the problem all along has been that the Western model of modernization that Western donors and bankers and African elites embraced was wholly inappropriate for Africa.

What is clear is that all the work of the development experts who have crisscrossed the continent over the past three decades, and all the initiatives—from donor governments, from the United Nations, from various foundations and think tanks—that have been put forward in their wake have not produced a model capable of lifting the majority of Africans out of the terrible poverty in which they find themselves. If the failure of the World Bank's controversial Structural Adjustment Initiative in the 1980s probably spelled the end of the old development model, the realization that humanitarian aid could both destabilize fragile societies, as arguably it did in Somalia in 1992, or contribute to the prolongation of war, as seems to have happened over the last decade in Sudan, left those eager to help in a quandary. Development had been a false dawn; so had humanitarianism. But the question of what to put in their place remained. The needs have not gone away. They are as pressing today as they were when the basic structures of development assistance were erected in the 1960s.

Ironically, some, including James Gustave Speth, the former head of the United Nations Development Programme (UNDP), have suggested that aid flows are being cut back at precisely the moment when what Speth called "an effective new architecture of development cooperation" has been put in place. The United Nations, of course, along with the Netherlands and the Nordic countries, has long been Africa's most reliable and impassioned advocate. Not for nothing did the late Anthony Parsons, the former British ambassador to the United Nations, dub the world organization a great "decolonization machine."

But however much UN officials have tried to persuade major donor governments that, as Speth put it, development aid is surely "the price we should willingly pay to live in a civilized or civilizing world," such views carry even less weight today than they did in the past, in part because the memory of colonialism has largely faded, and with it the residual appeal of the West's guilty conscience. The mere fact that an increasingly impotent and financially derelict United Nations has been Africa's court of last resort offers eloquent proof of the continent's marginalization. Over the last two decades, where Africa has been concerned the United Nations has gone from being a decolonization machine to an alleviation machine, unable to do much, as the term itself implies, to address the underlying causes of the African calamity.

THE LOST CONTINENT

SECRETARY-generals could warn about events in Africa—Boutros Boutros-Ghali said it risked becoming "the lost continent"—but little has been achievable in practical terms. The New Agenda for the Development of Africa and the Tokyo International Conference on African Development are only the latest in a long line of initiatives with little or no prospect of making an appreciable difference in many African lives. All the talk about the world's shared responsibility for Africa falls on deaf ears these days, or, worse, in an era of lachrymose politicians like Bill Clinton and Tony Blair, eager to demonstrate to all and sundry how deeply they feel everyone's pain, what we see and hear are sympathetic statements and almost no concrete help. Moreover, the enduring expectations of many African leaders that one of these days Western governments will come to view the colonial period as imposing some special obligations not only have been counterproductive but have served as a smoke screen for many dictators to mask their own crimes and ineptitude.

The Dutch and the Scandinavian governments have bucked this trend to a considerable degree, agreeing to increase their official development assistance budgets to 1 percent of annual national GNP. But for the most part, donor governments have tended more and more to write off development aid as being at best an unsatisfactory stopgap and to insist that first the Africans must look to themselves.

Interestingly, by the mid-1980s, many African political leaders and commentators themselves had begun to draw similar conclusions. Blaming the West had become the dodge of military dictators and local demagogues, and as such it steadily lost credibility as a catchall explanation for Africa's woes. Already in 1978, Edem Kodjo, the former secretary-general of the Organization of African Unity, declared that "Africa is dying." What was taking place before everyone's eyes could no longer be denied. In 1986, in his book, *The Africans,* Ali Mazrui wrote that "things are not working out in Africa. From Dakar to Dar es Salaam, from Marrakesh to Maputo, institutions are decaying, structures are rusting away." The political reaction, particularly once apartheid South Africa, the last bastion of white supremacy on the continent, had fallen, was not long in coming. In 1992, Nelson Mandela remarked that many Africans "are irate at their leaders for having betrayed them." Not long after, the Ugandan leader, Yoweri Museveni, looking back on the legacy of dictatorship, corruption, economic stagnation, war, and poverty, said that Africa had "lost thirty years to the sergeants."

MARKETING AFRICA

AND IF this was true, then the question was whether, now that in at least some African societies people were facing their problems squarely, there was a way out for the continent. In all societies, there is a lag time between diagnosis and the first efforts at cure. But in a surprisingly short period of time, a very different approach to African problems was adopted in countries from Mali to

Burkina Faso, and from Uganda to Botswana. And almost overnight, it became possible for a reasonable person to believe that the Afro-pessimism of most of the last two decades, seemingly so firmly grounded in African reality, might be giving way to something more hopeful. Despite the atrocities of the Rwandan genocide and the ongoing war in Sudan, the meltdown of Zaire and the deliquescence of the Kenyan political order, the first good news from Africa in a very long time has begun to make itself known. Slightly grandiloquently perhaps, Thabo Mbeki, the South African deputy president, could argue that Africa stood poised on the verge of a "renaissance."

In Mbeki's view, after so many false dawns, the turning point had finally come in Africa. Neither he nor the many African politicians and scholars, UN officials, and other foreign well-wishers denied the scope of the continent's problems. But they argued that the future was filled with opportunity. African leaders, they insisted, had finally recognized that they had to be the agents of change in their own society, and the soldiers who had ruled for so long were seeing the handwriting on the wall. Democratic elections were being held; military regimes were being dismantled; and a new and energetic civil sector of business groups, nongovernmental organizations, and independent media were coming into their own. A reconfiguration of the relations between the state and society, one in which the former would no longer simply prey on the latter, seemed underway, not just in a few countries along the South African border, but in many countries across the continent.

The undeniable fact that these social transformations were soon accompanied by demonstrable improvements in at least some economic indicators, above all a rise in growth rates, made it possible for the first time in a generation to entertain the entrancing vision of an Africa that was being remade both in the sense of business opportunities for foreign investors—the hard fact of our post-Thatcherite times being that without that prospect the rich world rarely pays attention to the poor world for long—but also in the important and constructive sense of a rosier destiny for the peoples of Africa. All of Africa might still be poor, the argument went, and parts of the continent might still be in crisis, but with the end of the neocolonial, patrimonial state the last years of the twentieth century were also a time of tremendous promise.

An emblematic expression of this view can be found in the spring 1998 issue of *World Policy Journal.* In an article titled "The Other Africa: An End to Afro-pessimism," David Gordon, a senior fellow at the Overseas Development Council, and former congressman Howard Wolpe, President Clinton's special representative to the Great Lakes region of Africa, wrote of an African renewal, fueled by both political and economic reform and led by a new generation of leaders committed to the democratization of their own societies, that had already yielded "a new sense of hope and possibility." The ingrained Afro-pessimism in Western Europe and North America, they insisted, was based on ignorance and racial stereotyping, as well as on media coverage influenced both by these same biases and a tropism toward negative stories, and had little to do with contemporary African realities. "While Africa remains the poorest continent in the world," Gordon and Wolpe wrote, "a number of African countries are already reaping the fruits of new market-oriented institutions and policies."

Beyond the factors of improving economic indicators and political democratization, their optimism, and that of the many outside observers who have expressed similar views in conferences and journal articles, is also grounded in the belief that the end of the Cold War may finally have put an end to Africa as battlefield—a condition that, in and of itself might have sufficed to stymie development in the subcontinent. They have insisted, rightly in my view, that one of the reasons the fledgling states of postcolonial Africa never fulfilled the promise of the immediate period after the departure of the British and the French was that they had been enlisted, whether by the United States and its allies or by the Soviets, as proxies in the Cold War.

Today, however, the great powers—even, in the aftermath of the Rwandan genocide, the French, for whom maintaining a francophone African sphere of influence was vital to the claim that France remained a world power—are no longer so wedded to their local clients. This has left the political field open to local leaders who have either vied for power peacefully, as in Mozambique, or violently, as in Uganda, where Museveni started an insurrection in the bush without fearing that his effort to overthrow the Obote dictatorship would engender opposition in Washington or Moscow. In other words, the days when the road to democracy in Africa was routinely blocked by the CIA and the KGB seem to be ending.

ANOTHER FALSE DAWN

UNFORTUNATELY, for all the promising signs that could lead an African or a sympathetic foreign observer to believe in the reality of an "African Renaissance," it is far more likely that the new "Afro-optimism" is, tragically, yet another false dawn, based on little more than some promising but unrepresentative social developments, a move toward formal democracy that has not and shows no real promise of being translated into grass-roots democracy, a brief and transient spike in Africa's economic fortunes, and a vast overestimation of the qualities and commitment to democracy of a new generation of African rulers who, however different stylistically they are from their predecessors, are cut from very much the same basic mold—the African "Big Man."

Here, African continuities are at least as striking as African discontinuities. It should be remembered, at a time when journalists and area specialists are trumpeting Africa's new generation of leaders, that an earlier generation—Léopold Senghor in Senegal, William V. S. Tubman in Liberia, Kwame Nkrumah in Ghana, and Sékou Touré in Guinea—received many of the same plaudits from outside observers. That alone should engender a certain caution. The fact that the leaders most often praised by Afro-optimists—Museveni in Uganda, Paul Kagame in Rwanda, Jerry Rawlings in Ghana—came to power either in coups or after a military campaign should be further cause for skepticism. Their talk of free markets and democratic openings should certainly not be taken at face value. Some may be sincere, but it cannot be overstressed that in this age of global capitalism's high-water mark, this is the talk donors now demand.

In any case, the outlook for an African revival does not depend all that much on whether or not men like Rawlings or Museveni are sincere. Afro-optimists would concede that even the most positive cases of economic and political turnaround, which, in any case, look considerably less promising at the end of 1998 than they did in the middle of 1997, have occurred (with the exception of the admittedly anomalous case of South Africa) in small countries in subregions where the larger countries are in desperate trouble.

Uganda may be doing well by some criteria, but its much larger neighbor, Kenya, on which it remains economically dependent, is in free fall. Ghana has made considerable progress, but the situation of Senegal has deteriorated gravely in the past ten years. Surely the most fervent Afro-optimist would be hard-pressed to make the case that most of the largest African countries are making progress. When Nigeria, the Democratic Republic of Congo, Sudan, Kenya, and Angola are either in economic or political turmoil or actually at war, it is difficult to see how small neighboring states will somehow manage to shrug off the ripple effect. In terms of refugee flows alone, a crisis in one of the large states would almost certainly undo the progress of half a dozen smaller ones.

Moreover, the successes of those states that have shown progress are only relative, as the Afro-optimists know perfectly well. After pointing to Ghana and Uganda as two of the most promising stories on the continent, Gordon and Wolpe note in passing that "neither country is back to where it was 25 years ago." Again, it is possible that the transformation of at least some African states has been real. But without sustained economic growth, and some insulation from war, refugee flows, and humanitarian emergencies, it is open to question how long-lived these transformations will be.

Most important, what the optimistic view of Africa's prospects often glosses over is the degree to which all the transformations of the past decade were based on the assumption that it was feasible and desirable for Africa to be integrated into the world economy, and that the political and economic interest among rich countries in assisting in this process could be mobilized.

To a certain extent, the claims of Afro-optimists can be viewed as a kind of marketing effort for Africa—part of the campaign to secure commitments from the rich world and overcome the negative images of Africa that are, as Gordon and Wolpe rightly point out, often the only ones Western audiences are exposed to. Not by accident did Thabo Mbeki first formally employ the term "African Renaissance" at a speech to the Corporate Council on Africa's "Attracting Capital to Africa" conference held in Chantilly, Virginia, in April 1997. To be sure, the boosterism, which viewed in a certain light is no different from that of any American elected official pitching his or her region to a business group, comes freighted with other appeals and admonitions. More often than not, talk of the reality of the African Renaissance segues rapidly into accusations that to deny its reality is racist, and into assertions that whatever the economic prospects, there are moral obligations involved—a view with which, incidentally, I concur fully. But it is one thing to insist that we ignore Africa at our moral and their physical peril, and quite another to claim that things have taken such a radical turn for the better there.

Humanly, of course, this claim is not simply understandable; it does credit to the moral sensitivities of those who advance it. No decent person enjoys being pessimistic, nor should pessimism be wielded like a club, as it so often has been in the past by outsiders eager to write off Africa and to preclude engagement with the continent's problems. And yet the proponents of Africa's renewal have based their optimism on a set of assumptions not just about Africa but about the world in general that do not hold up well on closer examination. In particular, the American version of this Afro-optimism seems to stem as much from important domestic policy considerations and from still deeper American preconceptions about how to address difficult political questions as it does from any profound understanding of the problems that will bedevil all efforts to mitigate the African crisis.

The domestic policy issues are obvious enough. President Clinton's dependence on African-American voters made both his visit to Africa in 1997 and the support he has repeatedly given to the idea that Africa is becoming again a region of great promise and opportunity a sound political move. In this sense—and, if anything, it is surprising how long it took for this to become a reality—Africa is simply taking its place as the latest international arena in which a U.S. president must be seen to be engaged for domestic political reasons, and Clinton's assertion that what he saw happening on the continent was—what else?—"the beginning of a new African renaissance" hardly needs to be taken at face value. The tour made political sense for the president, and political sense for the many African-American politicians who accompanied him and clearly found it to their advantage to be photographed with the president in the company of Uganda's Museveni.

None of this is either surprising or especially objectionable. But to confuse it with substantive changes in U.S. policy toward Africa, or to imagine that any real engagement is likely to be forthcoming is pure wishful thinking. Unlike the British government under Tony Blair, the Clinton administration has not made debt-forgiveness a public issue. The administration has supported one trade bill, the "African Growth and Opportunity Act." The bill is couched in the lofty language of a new U.S.-Africa partnership. In practical terms, however, though it makes some funds available to support private U.S. investment in the subcontinent and to underwrite the privatization of state-owned industries, the bill is unlikely to make much of a difference to any part of the region outside South Africa. Because of its "trade, not aid" emphasis, it may have the unintended consequence of lowering the total amounts of humanitarian and development aid African countries receive from the United States at a time when U.S. foreign aid is at an all-time low in percentage terms.

OPTIMISM AS A GOVERNING GENERALITY

In terms of direct U.S. political involvement on the continent, the Clinton administration's preference in the last year seems to have been to give the young assistant secretary of state for African affairs, Susan Rice, who is a protégée of Madeleine Albright, something of a free hand to formulate U.S. policy on the subcontinent. But the fact that an assistant secretary is making policy is eloquent proof of how marginal Africa is in U.S. calculations. And Rice's record is mixed at best. She failed to foresee the renewal of fighting between Ethiopia and Eritrea, and badly bungled U.S. policy in the Great Lakes through her uncritical support of the Kagame regime in Rwanda in its efforts first to install Laurent Kabila in Congo and then to overthrow him. In fairness, even had Rice done a better job, she would still have been operating—as Secretary Albright herself operates—in the context of an administration whose focus has always been principally centered on domestic issues.

In a sense, the real U.S. commitment is less to Afro-optimism than to optimism as a governing generality. For, as in so many other matters of public policy, where Africa is concerned that deep-seated American attitude that assumes that every problem can be solved, and that, all things being equal, tomorrow will be better than today, plays a not inconsiderable role. President

Clinton's emblematic phrase, "I still believe in a place called Hope," is relevant here. Indeed, if optimism is seen as a moral good—and most Americans do see it that way—and, more important, as part and parcel of any effort to combat a wrong or develop a new policy, then pessimism is itself a force, and a malign one at that. Obviously, the position of the Afro-optimists can hardly be reduced to such crude millenarian nominalism, or to the more conventional polemical interest of making their case one that is politically difficult to rebut. But the issue of belief is central in our society, where the commonplace assumption is that reality is there for the remaking.

The dangers of this view can be identified in many areas of American politics, from immigration policy to the way political candidates now run their campaigns. Where Africa is concerned, the truth can be occluded, but in the long run denying it in the name of some politically correct wish to be hopeful will do no one any good. For there is simply very little reason to be hopeful. Neither the political situation as it actually exists, nor the prospects for the kinds of transformations that will have to take place in Africa, give one any particular grounds for such hope.

It is possible, of course, simply to insist that one must hope for hope's sake, but in that case the debate acquires a metaphysical cast in which all questions of evidence and all reliance on probabilities have little relevance. Similarly, it is possible to make the case that it is important to pretend that things are going better, because otherwise the public in the rich world would lose whatever marginal interest it entertains in Africa. These may be correct judgments politically. They are, however, unsustainable intellectually. And surely if the situation in Africa is dire, and growing more dire by the day, then that needs to be said, not swept under the rug in the name of racial justice, or business opportunity, or simply the wish not to feel badly about a part of the world for which there are ample reasons to mourn and feel afraid.

Afro-optimism is hardly an American phenomenon alone. Indeed, its particular configuration, I think, has as much if not more to do with the triumphalism that succeeded the collapse of the Soviet empire as it does with the deep structures of America's feel-good politics. In Africa itself, it was not simply the shame and misery of the past but the triumph of free market economic arrangements all over the world, made manifest by the collapse of the Soviet empire and the end of the Cold War, that finally impelled a new generation of African leaders to reconsider their previous commitments. These beliefs, stemming as they did from the "state socialist" credos of so many of the founding generation of leaders who had led Africa to independence and of their Western allies, above all in Britain and Scandinavia, and at the United Nations, were revealed not so much as wrong than as irrelevant. In a world in which protected economies were not an option, and in which donor governments in the West were making continued aid dependent on democratic political openings and the establishment of free markets, responsible African leaders had little choice but to radically alter the way their societies were organized, even though the economic effects of protectionism and import substitution that predominated in much of Africa in the immediate postcolonial period were more mixed than is now commonly supposed.

CONVENTIONAL WISDOM

In any case, Africa's increasing dependence, in large measure because of the crushing burden of the continent's international debt, on the United Nations and the Bretton Woods institutions, made acquiescence to largely unfettered market arrangements pretty much of a foregone conclusion. Those countries that did not liberalize their trade and move toward democracy, however haltingly—states like Nigeria and Mobutu's Zaire, which had natural resources that were so valuable that they expected to be left alone—were vulnerable to having lines of credit halted. And the donors could do this with a clear conscience because, by the mid-1990s, it had become an article of faith in the rich world, and, later, with the ascension of Kofi Annan, the first UN secretary-general to appear to share the presuppositions of the globalizers, within the UN system, that open markets and democracy are the only possible avenues to prosperity. "No country can afford to opt out from the process of globalization under way," Annan has remarked. His view unquestionably represents the conventional wisdom of the end of the twentieth century.

It was a view that was refined during the early and mid-1990s; in other words, during the high-water mark of the East Asian miracle. And it had little patience for Afro-pessimism. Asia, Afro-optimists have often reminded their detractors, started from a similarly impoverished situation. Africa was best seen not as a zone of unextirpable misery, want, and war, but as an emerging market. And emerging markets were going to be the engines of growth in the twenty-first century. "Africa," in the emblematic observation of one South African entrepreneur, "is a huge market; it may be turbulent at times, but it eats and uses toiletries every day."

Viewed in this light, the implicit argument of the Afro-optimists was that it was impossible to be pessimistic about Africa because it was impossible, over the long term anyway, to be pessimistic about globalization. As Kofi Annan said, the globalized world is one in which opportunities "abound." Even in the short term, Africa's future was, if not assured, then certainly far from bleak—at least so long as Africans took steps to end the corruption and lack of democracy that was seen by Afro-optimists as having stifled Africa's development. To be sure, some of these arguments, notably on the part of UN officials, perhaps including Annan himself, can be seen as an effort to make the best of existing reality. After all, official development aid was being cut, and there was and remains little prospect that the trend will be reversed. Under those circumstances, what other hope was there for Africa except free trade?

And for a time, Africa's macroeconomic development seemed to bear out the Afro-optimists' scenario. The problem, though, is that during the last year that same process of globalization that the Afro-optimists had confidently predicted would lift the continent up has been the instrument of the undoing of much of the economic progress some countries in Africa saw during the middle of the decade. After the East Asian crash, Africa, with its ruined infrastructure (there are more telephones in Greater New York than there are between the Atlas mountains and Cape Town), its lack of an industrial base, its inefficient airports and harbors, its political instability, the high crime rates in its cities, and the threat of AIDS, which has imperiled many of the countries—Uganda, Botswana, Zimbabwe, Zambia, and South Africa—where economic and political developments have been most promising, could hardly compete with East Asian countries that were now aggressively lowering the already low cost of locating industries there. Not in a world economy from which a great deal of capital liquidity had suddenly been removed and much of which was on the edge of recession. The kind of speculative investment that, even at its best, Africa was always going to represent in at least the short and medium terms was no longer nearly as attractive as it had been previously.

In short, despite the reforms many African countries have put in place—what some African leaders call "the emerging environment of good government and free markets"—the economic bad news from Russia and East Asia may lead to a situation where there are few businesses interested in taking advantage of them. Globalization had always been a mixed blessing for Africa. Despite some moves on the part of the World Bank that were undertaken once James Wolfensohn took over and imparted to it some of his own moral scruples to begin to address the problem of debt relief, the debt burden of even favored African nations has not been reduced or has been reduced very little. There has been one initiative to reduce (though not forgive) the debt of a few so-called highly indebted poorer countries, and some moves to reward through debt-forgiveness and IMF loans and credits a few states favored by one or another great power, notably Uganda and Ivory Coast. But in the main, the effort to find solutions has neither been consistent nor imaginative.

GLOBALIZATION AS CATASTROPHE

AFRO-OPTIMISTS routinely argue that if Africa can only secure substantial investments, the continent will develop as Asia did. Presumably, they mean by this that African states will export their way out of their difficulties. Inside the continent, the dereliction of the infrastructure of most African nations makes trade difficult and expensive. Outside the continent, the picture is, if anything, even bleaker. On the macroeconomic level, the continent had already emerged a loser from the Uruguay Round of trade negotiations. The common economic policies of the European Union, destructive as they were of privileged markets in former colonial powers for African goods, have been a further blow. Without increased capital flows that go beyond traditional investments in the mining and energy sectors, as well as some liberalization of access of African goods to world markets—none of which now seems likely to occur in the near term, again because of the changed conditions of the global economy—the mixed blessing of globalization may well prove to be a disaster for the continent.

Though it does little good for the people of the continent, the debate about Africa actually offers a way of looking at globalization from a very different perspective—one in which its virtues are not simply stipulated. Increasingly, it appears that the major power shift in world affairs, from the public to the private, and from national governments to private corporations and international financial institutions, that we know as globalization, will prove to be catastrophic for Africa. Both Afro-optimists and -pessimists agree that the continent missed out on the benefits of the first wave of globalization, while avoiding none of its costs. The question now is whether it is realistic to hope for a second wave. If not, Africa will have been put at the mercy of the markets. As Robert Hormats, the vice chairman of Goldman Sachs, has put it, "The great beauty of globalization is that nobody controls it." But while that may be all very well for the winners, it is likely to be disastrous for the losers. And it seems increasingly likely that in this market-driven world Africa will indeed be the great loser.

WHO WILL PAY THE PRICE?

DEVELOPMENT needs to be undertaken if we want to live in a world of human rights, a decent world. But do we? Or, more exactly, are we in the rich world willing to pay the price for this? On form, the likelihood of this is slim. That is bad enough news for countries that have some meager hope of developing on their own. For Africa, which depends on bilateral development aid and whose elites really cannot envisage the kind of untrammeled, chaotic free market system that lies at the core of the current international economic system, the global economy offers no way out for ordinary people and marginalizes the continent as a whole.

It has been argued that Africa entered the world economy at the wrong time, too late to profit from a world economic system in which cheap labor offered a competitive advantage. Even in East Asia, however, the economic miracle turned out to be as much myth as reality. At least the Asian Tigers benefited from vast capital inflows from the West and from Japan. Those inflows were unable to cushion East Asia from a crisis in 1997 and 1998. But imagine the situation of Asia today without those capital flows: that, in a nutshell, is the situation in which Africa now finds itself.

Without capital inflows, there is certainly no way for Africa to compete. But even if the capital flows were forthcoming, in a world in which there is a surfeit of labor it is hard to see why any business would choose to set up in Africa when it could simply expand in Asia. The middle class in Africa is too small, the infrastructure too antiquated, and literacy rates among workers too low. This is what makes the claims of Afro-optimists both so fallacious and, however good their intentions, counterproductive. You do not alleviate vast human suffering with fine words. To the contrary, the fine words may well get in the way of the search for viable answers to Africa's problems. When the market proves to have failed, what solution will be left?

Emotionally, it may be a great relief to imagine that, at the eleventh hour, Africa's fortunes have taken such a radical turn for the better because of democratization and the embrace of market capitalism by a new generation of African leaders. Rationally, it makes no sense. The bitter truth is that Africa is not prepared for the world market; it cannot compete, and if it is forced to do so it will not do so successfully. And yet, in the name of a purblind optimism, that is what its friends are urging it to do.

NO CORNER TURNED

AGAIN, given how much bad news there had been from Africa over the preceding decades, it is hardly surprising that many people would want to believe that the corner had finally been turned. After all, the alternative was to imagine an Africa perpetually suffering, and for people of conscience that prospect was all but unbearable. The possibility that the market might be taking care of things that decades of development assistance had done little to alleviate, was bound to bedazzle. Of course, even those who advanced such views most enthusiastically understood perfectly well that things would have to break extremely well for this African renaissance to actually take place. The countervailing forces at work on the continent, above all the AIDS epidemic, the poverty that almost four decades of development assistance had done little to assuage, and a pattern of state decomposition and misgovernment that had made Africa the site of the majority of the wars taking place in the world during the 1990s, might be mitigated in time but for the foreseeable future would remain constants.

However nuanced, the portrait of the continent the new Afro-optimism draws is simply not borne out by reality. To insist on this point is not to denigrate the efforts of the Afro-optimists to garner support for initiatives on behalf of the continent; or to belittle the efforts some African leaders have made to transform their own societies. It is the fundamental false premise of Afro-optimism—a premise that often seems more akin to an article of religious faith than to an empirical conclusion based on a sober assessment of the available evidence—that Africa can compete on equal footing in the current global economy that makes its good intentions perilous.

For Africa is weak. There is nothing to be gained and much to be lost by pretending otherwise, or even that it has the potential to become stronger soon. Indeed, in a world in which information technology is creating an even greater gulf between haves and have-nots, Africa's technological underdevelopment—a gap that grows more and more difficult and expensive to bridge every year—may be the greatest obstacle of all.

To help Africa, then, will be enormously difficult. Unfortunately, those institutions and nations interested in improving the situation of the continent are themselves weak. It is only in the African context that a derelict institution like the United Nations, understood by those who know it well as a supine organization, could be viewed as a power center. And the fine talk of powerful states on behalf of Africa should not be taken at face value. Africa is marginal to the geostrategic concerns of most important rich countries, and marginal to the economic concerns of most multinational corporations except those engaged in oil extraction or mining. In short, while levels of development assistance continue to fall and the levels of African indebtedness continue to rise, foreign private investment is not taking up the slack and foreign political engagement is intermittent and inconsistent.

Anyone wanting to contrast the rhetoric of concern for Africa with the reality need only look at the contrast between the African situation and that of Bosnia-Herzegovina. After the Dayton peace agreements, development funds flooded into Bosnia. No one is saying that the development model is bankrupt in the Balkans. Moreover, on October 28, 1998, $1 billion of the $1.5 billion Bosnian debt was forgiven. This was described, quite correctly, as a necessary step if the great powers were to ensure Bosnia's recovery and prevent a new round of fighting. And yet somehow it is expected that sub-Saharan Africa, which spends 25 percent of its export earnings on debt service, will recover without similar relief. No one seriously doubts that what is a sine qua non of peace in the Balkans is also a sine qua non of peace and stability in Africa. What is preventing similar engagement in Africa are the vast sums involved and, perhaps more crucially, the fact that the political commitment to Africa does not exist, for all the easy talk of a continent-wide renewal and stern admonitions against Afro-pessimism.

The figures tell the story. They almost always do. The initiative to aid highly indebted poorer countries unquestionably represents a step in the right direction in terms of African debt relief. But not only is the process cumbersome, the actual debt-service ratios are far in excess of what any creditor would impose were it concerned with speeding economic recovery. The ratio of debt service to export revenue varies between 20 and 25 percent. This is a great improvement over the 708 percent ratio some nations labor under. Yet, by way of comparison, the 1953 London Agreement imposed a maximum debt-service ratio on post–Marshall Plan Germany of 5 percent.

WHAT IS TO BE DONE

To MAKE the claim that there is more reason to be an Afro-pessimist than to believe in the promise of an African renaissance is not, however, the same thing as saying that there is nothing to be done. Quite the contrary, it is evident that much could be done. But this would require both money—vastly more money than even the most optimistic advocates of African development are hoping will be made available—and making Africa a priority. To be sure, given the record of corruption among the elites in most sub-Saharan African countries, the idea of simply offering more money to Africa is one that may seem counterintuitive. And yet money is surely part of the solution. Even more important than money is commitment, but commitment made with a clear-eyed understanding of how grave the African situation really is. Africa's problems, particularly in light of the apocalyptic implications of the AIDS pandemic, are far likelier to grow worse in the next decade than to be ameliorated.

The answers to those problems will never be provided by the market. Rather, it is the notion of human need and moral obligation, the sense that not to help Africa is a moral scandal, not the notion of economic promise, that could just possibly provide the underpinnings for an African renaissance. This would involve not only a vast increase in aid flows but a systematic effort to protect Africa from the effects of a global economic system in which the deck is stacked against it. In other words, the only solutions that will work involve a return to development assistance, not a flight from it, although of course liberalizing the terms of trade for African exporters, and, above all, addressing the problem of debt relief—preferably through turning the debt into grants, as some African leaders have proposed—would also be important. Then and only then would a properly grounded Afro-optimism be sustainable and worth championing.

How likely is any of this? Unless one assumes that values like solidarity and compassion will take hold in the rich world, not likely at all. And yet the paradox is that these are the only motivations that could make Afro-pessimism as unwarranted as its critics pretend it already is.

POSTSCRIPT

I wish that I could retract what I wrote in this piece. But by any measure, it seems to me that the situation in Africa has gotten worse, not better, in the interim. Even the UN, that relentless font of purblind optimism, now concedes that its goals for both poverty reduction and bringing the AIDS pandemic under control are now unlikely to be met. And while there is poverty in much of the world and the spread of AIDS to India and the former Soviet Union is one of the greatest threats the world now faces, inevitably a worsening of poverty and of AIDS means a worsening of an already catastrophic situation in Africa. According to a recent report, life expectancy in Zambia is now about thirty-three, slightly more than half of what it was in 1960 at the end of the colonial era. And Zambia is anything but the worst case on the continent. Sometimes it is obscene to pretend there is no cause for despair. Auschwitz was such a case. I feared then and fear now that sub-Saharan Africa may be another.

LOST KOSOVO

PREFACE

Along with "A New Age of Liberal Imperialism," "Lost Kosovo" is the other frankly interventionist and neoimperialist piece that I have included in this collection. I do not repudiate its reportage or its account of either the Serbs or Macedonian Slavs who figure in it or its account of the clash between humanitarian and political imperatives. The co-optation of humanitarian action by great powers that reached its culmination in Afghanistan where U.S. Secretary of State Colin Powell told a gathering of relief officials from private voluntary agencies that they were part of America's "combat team" was first tried in earnest in Kosovo. Although I supported NATO intervention, and, indeed, spend a good part of the piece wrongly lamenting NATO's fecklessness in not pursuing that intervention more aggressively, I think the piece anatomizes these contradictions in a way that still stands up.

What doesn't stand up is my complacency about the moral or political character of the Kosovar groups fighting the Serbs or my belief that the Kosovan tragedy would end well if the Milosevic regime in Belgrade were forced to give up its hold on the province (as it eventually was). It may have been right, as one relief worker, my friend John Fawcett, claimed, that "Kosovo was a battle for the soul of humanitarian-

ism," in the sense that the ethnic cleansing the Serbs had planned for the Kosovar Albanians could only be combated with military force. But it was wrong to imagine that battle ended with "liberation."

To the contrary, what postwar Kosovo has demonstrated is that the Kosvar Albanians were just as efficient at ethnic cleansing as their Serb counterparts had been when Belgrade and Orthodoxy held the upper hand. Since 1999, something on the order of a quarter million Serbs and Roma have been forced to flee the province, all under the largely silent eye of United Nations and European Union officials who preferred to claim that things were largely progressing in the right direction. Only riots in the ethnically-divided Kosovan town of Mitrovica in 2004 and a devastating report on the ethnic cleansing issued by the Office of the UN High Commissioner for Refugees that same year forced the so-called international community to come clean.

But this in no way excuses my own blindness, years earlier, on this score. As in post-genocide Rwanda, the victims were ready, willing and able to become the victimizers when they got their turn. And by 1999, I should have known this.

DURING THE FIRST THREE WEEKS OF OPERAtion Allied Force, the skies over Albania were effectively closed to civilian air traffic. The Albanian government had seen in the Kosovo crisis both an obvious danger and an obvious benefit. The danger was that half a million Kosovar refugees were flooding into the country. The benefit was that, in the course of coping with that flow, the great powers finally would have to help rebuild Albania. And so, even before Brussels had made a formal request, the government announced that it was turning over its ports and airspace to NATO. Given that Rinas Airport in Tirana, the capital, functioned only in daylight, and the main port, Durres, bore a stronger resemblance to Tunis when it was controlled by the Barbary pirates than to Rotterdam or even Piraeus, this was, to put it mildly, a gift with strings attached. It also made my getting into Albania rather complicated.

Theoretically, it was possible to take a flight from Rome aboard a start-up carrier called Alb Air; but fellow journalists told me the availability of seats aboard the old Russian plane was always in doubt until the last minute. That left the port of Bari on Italy's Adriatic coast. There one could get a ferry, the SS *Palladio,* to Durres.

While getting a berth was no problem, the boarding process was Dante-esque. First, some 1,000 other passengers and I were crammed together in the small departure hall of the port for more than four hours after the ship had been due to sail. We were then made to inch our way onboard through its bowels more slowly than I had ever imagined possible. The reason for the delay became clear when I reached the main deck. A solitary Albanian customs agent was checking the documents of each traveler, one by one by one.

It soon became apparent that, in addition to transporting aid workers, Albanian families returning home, and foreign journalists, the SS *Palladio* was, for all intents and purposes, a Kosovo Liberation Army (KLA) troopship. The volunteers, mostly young men from the Kosovar diaspora, came from as far away as the Bronx and Toronto and from as near as southern Italy. They boarded last, slept on the deck, and, the following morning, as the *Palladio* entered Albanian waters, were mustered by their officers for a political lecture before disembarking.

At quayside, they lined up once again in their Swiss Army surplus forest camouflage uniforms, young men still playing at being soldiers. "UCK!" (the Albanian acronym for Kosovo Liberation Army), they roared in unison, brandishing their fists. Drivers for the International Committee of the Red Cross, who had been stuck in the port for a day, looked down curiously from their cabs. Then the volunteers boarded buses and roared off toward their training camps.

"No more talk," a volunteer from Toronto, who the night before had told me that his father owned a pizzeria, called out exuberantly as he passed. To which a middle-aged Albanian, his pretty five-year-old granddaughter in one arm and a boxed toaster oven in the other, muttered in surprisingly good English, "Cannon fodder. The Serbs will cut them to pieces."

But the posturing of the volunteers, who, as I would later learn, were arriving on every ferry from Italy, was a sideshow. The real action in the port that day, as it was every day, was the aid effort. White vehicles were everywhere. They bore the logos familiar to anyone who has been in Bosnia, Rwanda, Liberia, or any of the other recent sites of humanitarian catastrophe—Caritas, Doctors Without Borders, Doctors of the World, Oxfam, and Catholic Relief Services, to name only a few. As Pete Spink, the able, young British director of the Albanian program of yet another major relief agency, the International Rescue Committee, put it, "You know it's a major disaster in the eyes of the world when the white vehicles begin to outnumber the local Mercedes!"

He might have added that you also know this when the international press is almost as thick on the ground as the relief workers. Indeed, the two often operate symbiotically. After all, aid is at once the ultimate expression of altruism and a fiercely competitive business. As the International Rescue Committee's John Fawcett, perhaps the most experienced and certainly the most innovative aid worker dealing with Kosovo, explains, "The received wisdom is the idea of market share; you go where governments or UN agencies want you to go to get your share of contracts that otherwise would go to other agencies." And one way to get such contracts—though not by any means necessarily the way Fawcett likes to operate—is by getting the press to publicize your work.

The various national branches of Doctors Without Borders pioneered this technique in the late 1970s and early 1980s. Other agencies soon followed suit. Today, all the major agencies involved in the Kosovo crisis have press officers. To hear each of them talk, you would barely imagine that any other agency was doing anything. And yet, for the relief agencies' efforts, in the Kosovo crisis, more than in any other previous humanitarian disaster, these international private voluntary organizations have acted more like subcontractors to the Office of the United Nations High Commissioner for Refugees (UNHCR), to the U.S. Agency for International Development, to its European opposite number, the European Commission Humanitarian Office, and, above all, to NATO.

It is NATO that has built the camps for the refugees as they pour into Albania and Macedonia. It is NATO that has guarded the refugees from bandits in northern Albania which is known as Albania's Appalachia, though it boggles the mind that so poor a country could contain within itself that much poorer a region. And it is NATO that has protected the refugees in Macedonia by serving as a buffer between the Kosovars and the ethnic Macedonians—for whom the arrival of so many ethnic Albanians represents a radical demographic shift in favor of that country's Albanian minority.

NATO's emergence as the preeminent aid organization in the crisis marks a radical departure from previous norms and is largely due to the UNHCR's failure to perform this role. In Bosnia, the UNHCR had distinguished itself—particularly under its first special envoy, José María Mendiluce—by breaking with its previous, rather cautious norms, and attempting, with great creativity and courage, to mitigate the humanitarian disaster as it unfolded and to bear witness to the atrocities of Serb (and later Croat) ethnic cleansing. No other UN agency had either as intelligent or as principled a view of the Bosnian conflict.

But in the case of Kosovo the agency was caught completely off guard. Many in the aid community privately grumbled that the UNHCR's unpreparedness was all the more inexcusable given its previous experience in the region. "For Christ's sake," says one aid worker, "they'd been dealing with Balkan wars for the entire eight years they'd been going on. But they pre-positioned supplies outside Kosovo for no more than a hundred thousand refugees, refused to distribute material like plastic sheeting inside Kosovo for people who might become internally displaced, and exerted almost no political pressure and sounded no alarms. As for staff, it was the UN bureaucracy at its worst—a bunch of time-servers whose main ambition seemed to be to reassure their superiors in Geneva that everything was under control; in other words, a bunch of fucking ostriches, Lords of Poverty variety."

Other UN agencies have been similarly slow-moving, as illustrated by the announcement by an official of the UN Development Program, two weeks after the bombing campaign had started, that his group was now "looking to do a longer impact study" of the effect of the refugee inflow on Albania. Meanwhile, many U.S. government aid grandees in Tirana remained holed up in their comfortable hotels forbidden by the State Department to travel in Albania except with large security details, owing to the supposed threat from groups loyal to Osama bin Laden and other Islamic fundamentalist terrorists.

UNHCR officials who have stuck it out from the start of the crisis in places like Kukes in northeastern Albania, a town of 25,000 that is the point of arrival for the bulk of the hundreds of thousands of Kosovar refugees to cross into Albania, are quick to point out that they, at least, are in the thick of the action. And they note that the UNHCR was not the only group that failed to anticipate the extent of the crisis. "I can't remember a single newspaper or TV reporter predicting Milosevic would ethnically cleanse all of Kosovo," says Ray Wilkinson, the organization's press officer in Kukes. "We were surprised along with the rest of the world." Furthermore, adds another UNHCR official, "Yes, we fucked up initially, but we're doing better today. We have a new team, including a new special envoy, and we are trying to sort out what went wrong."

It is easy to see how in a place like Kukes anything that could go wrong would go wrong. It is a miserable town, a lawless badland in what could have been beautiful mountain country, if the water table and the lake had not been hopelessly polluted by the coal and chromium mines that once fueled the region's economy. There have been almost no jobs in the region since these mines were closed. Although in most of Albania the refugees have been greeted with open arms—WELCOME, KOSOVAR BROTHERS AND SISTERS, reads the sign over the sports center that is now a refugee transit center in Tirana—the hospitality of Kukes has been understandably grudging at best.

The town is awash in petty crime, the roads are dangerous at night, and the infrastructure hasn't so much collapsed as it never existed in the first place. There is something of Mobutu's Zaire about the place, and something of Central Asia, both in its clan-ridden and in its Soviet police-state aspects. The KLA is everywhere. If a NATO ground war is ever launched, it will go from Kukes. (Of course, this is more wishful thinking on the part of aid workers and journalists—many of whom have lived through two of Slobodan Milosevic's wars of ethnic cleansing already—than a realistic prediction.) But, even if there is no ground war, the area will serve as a KLA staging ground for as long as Serb forces continue to operate in Kosovo.

Some of the camps are extremely well-run, even opulent by refugee standards, like one built by the Italian Army that has a full medical center, and Port-o-san-style toilets more appropriate for an outdoor rock concert in Umbria than a refugee emergency. Others are appalling, like the now-closed camp in an abandoned chicken farm in Kruma, north of Kukes. But the broader issue is not about which camp is better or even whether people should be moved away from the northern border region into camps further south in Albania. The real question is whether the refugee emergency is going to be permanent—the millennium's answer to the UN Relief and Works Agency camps in the Middle East of the late 1940s—or whether NATO actually intends to fight a war that will allow the refugees to return home to Kosovo.

And the outlook is not promising. The aid agencies are operating in an entirely new environment. But, then again, so is NATO. Although they are hurt and upset by the criticism that has been leveled against them, UNHCR officials, at least privately, are beginning to face the fact that, whatever happens, they will probably go out losers from the Kosovo crisis. NATO and its member governments seem to have not yet come to grips with the fact that the same future probably awaits them. In Skopje, I ran into an old friend from the foreign press corps in Sarajevo. He had been away for several months and was just returning.

"What's going on?" he asked.

I told him that I had been up at the crossing from Kosovo into Macedonia; the Macedonian border guards had been behaving with even more offhanded cruelty than usual, forcing refugees who had seen their relatives butchered to remain cooped up for hours in buses with neither water nor toilet facilities. The UNHCR, try as it might, could do nothing about this for the better part of the day. "We're losing this war," I said.

"Tell me something I don't know," he said flatly. But that's not the punch line. This is: An official of the U.S. Embassy in Skopje had been standing nearby. "I don't know how you guys can talk that way," he said. "We're winning this thing. And I believe we will see it through!

"From your mouth to God's ear," I said.

"From the people who brought you the Dayton Agreement and said it was a victory for American resolve and democratic values," a colleague who had been eavesdropping said after the diplomat had moved away.

Even then, three weeks ago, it was clear that the mass deportations of the Kosovars were going to continue until there were just enough ethnic Albanians left in Kosovo to create a humanitarian obstacle—in the literal as well as the figurative sense—to any NATO ground attack. For the time being, expelling Kosovars was not just something the Serb soldiers, policemen, and paramilitaries could do with impunity; it was good business. There was even an informal price list. This fact tended to get lost, for understandable reasons, in the newspaper and television accounts of what the refugees had gone through. When someone tells you she saw her husband get his throat cut, you tend to pay less attention to the fact that the murderers also demanded 1,000 Deutsche marks per child so that she could take the rest of her family on the road toward Albania.

And yet it may well turn out that greed played a huge role in the willingness of ordinary Serbs to participate in Operation Horseshoe—Slobodan Milosevic's plan, concocted almost a year before the current crisis, for a "final solution" to the "problem" of the ethnic Albanians. One of the greatest hidden dynamics of the Kosovo crisis, at least as powerful as any history of ethnic antipathy (though, unlike Bosnia, that did exist in Kosovo), has been not only that the Kosovars were more prosperous than their Albanian cousins—every one in Europe is richer than the Albanians, even the Macedonians and Moldovans—but that they were richer than their Serb neighbors in the province as well. To expel them was to have a chance at their television sets, their gold rings, and their cash.

The chance at loot, as well as the operational necessity of making sure they did not stray too far from the corridors toward the border along which the Serbs were pushing them, explains why the Kosovars were robbed in their homes and robbed at the border (as well as stripped of the identity documents, property deeds, and marriage and birth certificates they would need were they to return) but were largely left alone during the march out of Kosovo. Obviously, the NATO bombing is a catastrophe for the prosperity of Serbia. But that is in the long run, which is a measurement that ordinary Serbs proved incapable of considering when they supported first the war in Croatia, then the war in Serbia. In the short run, a lot of Serb fighters, or just ordinary Serbs with an eye for a quick Deutsche mark, are making a lot of money from the Kosovars as they expel them. That alone makes Milosevic's task far easier than it might have been otherwise.

Those Kosovars who remain might serve as a buffer against a NATO attack. There will be no Desert Storm in Kosovo, even in the unlikely eventuality that NATO summons the will to launch the ground war. If NATO attacks, it will face a human wall of Kosovars between it and the Serb forces. It has been difficult enough to cope with the demographic bomb that Milosevic launched on Macedonia by sending the ethnic Albanian Kosovar refugees into a country whose dominant ethnic group was already pro-Serb and fearful of the Albanian minority within. In Kosovo, the situation would be exponentially worse.

"NATO is not in the business of meals on wheels; it should be in the business of guns and missiles," an American officer told me in Skopje. "But it will take two or three months for a ground war to get going, and the American people are not going to go for it. In the meantime, Milosevic will probably try to spread this thing into Albania, Montenegro, and, above all, right here in Macedonia. Everyone knows the Macedonians don't want anyone in the country."

If anything the situation was worse than he was saying. The night before, I had gone to a rock concert in the main square of Skopje—Macedonia Square, or, as some older residents of the city persist in calling it, Tito Square. The concert was a virtual clone of the anti-NATO concerts going on in Belgrade and other Serb cities at the time. Here, though, the crowd was not Serb but overwhelmingly Macedonian. It was a beautiful night, full of what my rock-and-roll-besotted friends in Sarajevo during the siege would have called "good energy." Handsome boys and good-looking girls stood pressed together in the vast crowd, swaying to the music when it was soft and lyrical or dancing frenetically when it was driving. At the edges stood families with small children. The vendors were doing a good business. There was something so benign and attractive about it all, it could have been a Balkan Woodstock. Plenty of things about the Balkans make you feel you are in a time warp, why not that?

But, of course, it wasn't Woodstock, 1969. If you want a comparison, try Nuremberg, 1936. The hands waving in the air were not making the V sign of peace but the three-fingered salute of Serb nationalism. They brandished American flags where the stars were swastikas or the ubiquitous target signs that have now migrated from the Balkans to Beijing. ADOLPH CLINTON, the signs read, and NATO MURDERERS. The slogan, WE ARE ALL TARGETS, reflected the depth with which—never mind Vukovar, never mind Srebrenica, never mind what was happening in Kosovo—at that very moment those in the crowd felt themselves the victims.

War and Yugonostalgia, Serb nationalism and anti-Americanism; they made for a heady mix that night. The quality of the music was high; the energy was fantastic; the crowd was terrifying. "Yugoslavia, Yugoslavia," they shouted between songs. "Peace in the Balkans, peace for all!" a well-known Macedonian singer called Rebecca shouted. "Milosevic! Peace! Milosevic! Peace!" the crowd shouted back.

Earlier, I had heard an official of the German branch of the Catholic aid organization Caritas observe wonderingly, "It's much worse than I thought. I believe we will have a civil war here in Macedonia soon. Everyone is getting ready—the KLA, Milosevic's people, the Macedonians. It's like a gasoline lake. I am very surprised, but I am sure."

• • •

AT THE TIME, I had thought he was exaggerating. After the concert, I was less certain. And yet both U.S. State Department officials and NATO military officials, who have consistently downplayed attacks on their own personnel and the vandalism of their vehicles, seemed strangely unperturbed. "Why is this operation being judged so quickly?" a member of U.S. Ambassador Christopher Hill's staff asked a group of journalists plaintively. A more senior official, whom human rights activists unfailingly cite as one of the most scrupulous and conscience-ridden within the department, said more or less the same thing during a lightning visit to Skopje.

"Why are you so sure it's a failure?" he asked.

Because, one reporter told him, the results of the bombing have amounted to increased refugee flows, the beginning of the destabilization of Macedonia, and the destruction of modern Serbia. The official could barely contain his exasperation. "It's a process," he said, as evenly as he could. "We don't yet know how it will end."

Some U.S. diplomats put their faith in the influence of John McCain and other pro-war Republicans in Washington. Others take hope in the conviction that NATO simply couldn't lose the first war it had chosen to fight in its fifty-year history. The American officer I met in Skopje was betting on the Apache attack helicopters: They were being brought into Albania just at that time. "The Apaches are going to turn the corner on this," he told me. "They're going to turn this into a different war with the average Serb soldier experiencing," he grinned, "a much more interesting life."

His enthusiasm was as contagious as his arguments were unconvincing. Having predicted a radical change on the battlefield, he went on to predict a deepening of the humanitarian crisis. "There's going to be as big a refugee crisis inside Kosovo as there is outside now," he said, "and that's assuming we go in after an agreement. Its magnitude could be triple what we face now." He paused. "Maybe that's Milosevic's plan—to rubber band the crisis back into Kosovo.'

When I repeated this later to an aid-worker friend, he just shook his head. Already by late April, it had become clear that only Milosevic had a strategy. What NATO, the international organizations, and the aid agencies had was a wish list and a set of tasks and mandates, many of which put them at cross purposes with one another. The UNHCR worried that NATO's dominance in the relief operation would destroy its autonomy and its ability to perform its refugee protection functions, which, after all, was the organization's original purpose. As Ray Wilkinson put it, "We worry that NATO may take over everything, both the military and civilian roles." But, he added, "If we don't turn to NATO, who in do we turn to?"

For its part, NATO was fighting a war that, if the historical precedents of other bombing campaigns—World War II Germany, Vietnam, post–Desert Storm Iraq—were indicative, was unlikely to force Milosevic to give in. NATO officials buried themselves in detail and found, to the surprise of many and the discomfiture of some, that building and administering refugee camps was something they did extremely well. But in the final analysis their success was an emblem of their military failure. An operation whose original stated aim was to forestall ethnic cleansing, and is still supposedly dedicated to reversing it, is now principally involved with caring for refugees who are unlikely to return home. Indeed, by this stage of the game the food and shelter of the refugee camps may have turned into a magnet drawing more and more people out of their blasted villages in Kosovo.

The rule of thumb among refugee officials is that a refugee who stays away for more than a year or two is unlikely to return. And yet, by moving refugees away from the Albanian border (for their safety), or submitting to some extent to the Macedonian government's demand that a refugee be resettled outside Macedonia for every refugee that is let in (to forestall a political explosion), NATO is doing exactly what it least wants to. It is accepting the role of guardian of the refugees and, to an increasing degree, contributing to the ethnic cleansing. This dilemma was one the International Committee of the Red Cross already faced in northern Bosnia in 1992, and, like NATO today, it chose to facilitate the Muslims' departures. But everyone knows now, as everyone knew then, however much we choose to focus on the family reunions and the kindness of U.S. soldiers in the resettlement camp in New Jersey, that the choice is an unspeakable one.

TO ALLOW the refugees to continue to rot in camps is unacceptable. But to resettle refugees in the United States or Canada or Switzerland or Britain, however decent or practical a gesture, is to convert the refugees into exiles. These Kosovars are joining well-established immigrant communities; they are going to stay in the West, as most of us would if we were in their shoes; many were trying to get there before the crisis. And so Slobodan Milosevic will have his way, as he did in Bosnia—where the single greatest failure of the post-Dayton period, apart from not arresting Radovan

Karadzic and Ratko Mladic, has been that almost no refugees have returned to areas where they do not belong to the dominant ethnic group. The demography of Kosovo will be changed through our good offices as well as Milosevic's murderous intent.

Obviously, were NATO seriously contemplating a ground war, a more sanguine view would at least be defensible. And, even with a NATO victory, the problems would be close to insurmountable, at least in the short term. As John Fawcett put it, "We already know that, when the Serbs leave, they will blow up every water plant and poison every well. You will have a combination of a security risk and a humanitarian crisis. Our people who are fighting the war will have to cope with a humanitarian crisis at the same time."

Under the circumstances, the surprise might be that the Clinton administration has shown as much backbone as it has. But, as a member of the Kosovar Albanian delegation to the Rambouillet talks put it to me bitterly, "It seems as if NATO and Milosevic increasingly have the same interest: to end the bombing and bring the war to a close as quickly as possible."

One way to move toward this end without appearing to do so would be to "humanitarianize" the crisis; that is, to begin to talk about innocent victims and, by implication, to argue that the rights and wrongs of the dispute are secondary. That, to some extent, is what Jesse Jackson has been trying to do since his return from Belgrade. The reappearance on center stage of the United Nations and Kofi Annan, who more or less wrote the book on this tactic in Bosnia, suggests that just such a move is in the offing. Since then, Yasushi Akashi, the UN special representative who found nothing much to choose morally between the Bosnian Serbs and the Sarajevo government, has visited Belgrade and smilingly repeated for the press, as he did so often during the Bosnian war, the current Serb position. For those of us who were in Bosnia, the sight was sickening beyond words.

The point, of course, as Fawcett said to me in Tirana, is that "this is not a humanitarian crisis; this is a political crisis." Having lived through the siege of Sarajevo, Fawcett has the gravest doubts about the humanitarian's proper role. "This is our last chance," he said. "The Kosovo crisis is a battle for our soul, the soul of humanitarianism."

For Fawcett, the solution is clear: Milosevic must be routed. "When fascism goes violent," he said, "you must use violence." But, despite the efforts of people like Fawcett to galvanize their fellow aid workers and the NATO governments in a different direction, and to make clear that humanitarian aid cannot be used, as it was in Bosnia, as a fig leaf for political cowardice, there is disgrace in the air, both in Washington and Brussels and on the ground in Macedonia and Albania. In the long run, it is almost inevitable that an independent Kosovo will come into being. The stupidest thing about this stupid war is that, for all their talk of primordial attachment to Kosovo, almost no Serb actually wants to live there. So, in the end, if NATO does not see things through, the KLA will. But thousands if not tens of thousands more people will be killed and the prospects of a democratic Kosovo all but extinguished. Meanwhile, the notion that a guerrilla army will eventually succeed where the largest and most powerful military alliance in the history of the world failed should be preposterous. But it is not.

GOODBYE, NEW WORLD ORDER

HERE IS THE PESSIMISTS' CASE: WHATEVER ELSE it may eventually accomplish, the war in Iraq seems to have put the final nail in the coffin of the dream of global citizenship that began more than half a century ago with the founding of the United Nations. Instead of a world order grounded, however imperfectly, in the idea of collective security, the war has made plain one of the central new realities of the post-9/11 world: the most powerful nation on earth, the United States of America, has decided to turn the international system on its head.

That system was based on strong states committing themselves not to do everything that was in their power. They did not make such undertakings out of altruism (states are states, after all, not charitable trusts), but out of the insight born in the ashes of World War II that the benefits of multilateralism far outweighed its risks. The Nazi experience showed that the right to act unilaterally was bound to be abused by evil regimes and provided democracies with insufficient means to confront evil. The organizers of the United Nations, notably such distinguished Americans as Franklin

Delano Roosevelt, Eleanor Roosevelt, and Ralph Bunche, in effect tried to constrain all nations within the legal steel hawsers of a doctrine of collective security.

In reality, this system never worked very well. War might have been outlawed under the UN Charter (except in the case of self-defense or threats to collective security), but throughout the Cold War era, both the United States and the Soviet Union pursued their own interests, and, when they deemed it necessary, went to war, though usually by proxy and usually in the Third World. This alone probably should have been enough to convince anyone that the brave new norms of international conduct enshrined in such founding UN documents as the Charter and the Universal Declaration of Human Rights were nothing more than empty stipulations of collective moral ambitions. By any objective criterion, the world remained the same tragic place it had always been, as unredeemed by international law as it had been by religion or Marxism or liberal capitalism.

But such pessimism is unacceptable to most people except in the darkest of times. None of us wants to believe that there is no hope for a better world, any more than we want to believe that there is no hope for ourselves and our families. Americans are particularly drawn to a hopeful approach, in politics as in personal fulfillment—a faith in the notion that the present is better than the past and, even when it isn't, that the future beckons brightly.

Of course, it was not only such psychological and cultural predispositions that led the post-1945 generation to believe in the reality of an international community, and in the possibility of global democracy and global justice. It was a time when, in Western Europe and North America anyway, people became prosperous to a degree that would have been unimaginable at any previous moment in history; when campaigns for justice—labor rights, women's rights, the civil rights movement—seemed to have succeeded in overturning what many had considered the "natural" order of things. At such a time, why would it seem so unreasonable or unrealistic to dream of a world in which other "natural" conditions, most significantly war itself, were brought under control?

Today, not least because of Iraq, such expectations may seem preposterous, otherworldly. As a disenchanted friend of mine at the United Nations said to me recently, "We like to say at the UN that had the world organization not existed, the world would have to invent it. But we all know that people at the level of the founders of the UN don't exist in international politics at present. In other words, we *couldn't* invent it today." Indeed, with the possible exception of British Prime Minister Tony Blair, there is not a single head of state of a democratic country who seems genuinely committed to a set of principles that he or she is willing to risk career and future for (and this is not necessarily to endorse the particular principles Blair is committed to, only to honor him for hewing to them).

Yes, many people still want to believe in the United Nations—though they're becoming fewer and fewer in number. There is even the fantasy that some institutional or policy silver bullet—the International Criminal Court, say, or the Kyoto Protocol—will provide an Archimedean lever for solving the world's woes. Were it not for the machinations of the United States, which refused to sign on to either Kyoto or the international court, the argument goes, we would be well on our way to a better world; even so, America stands only as an obstacle that sooner or later will be overcome on the road to inevitable progress.

Such claims have all the ingredients of a fine press release, but the reality is more depressing. It is true, for example, that European governments increasingly subscribe to the ideology—some would say the secular religion—of human rights. But then so does the United States; after all, the official position of the U.S. government is that the intervention in Iraq was undertaken at least in part in the name of human rights. Now a doctrine that can be claimed by the United States of America as well as the still social democratic nations of Western Europe, and the nongovernmental organizations that view the United States as little more than a rogue state—not to mention major transnational corporations that have signed on to a UN "compact with business"—has become elastic to the point of fatuousness. If we all claim to be pledged to the cause of human rights (and who, it seems, does not?), then it is hard not to think of Dr. Johnson's remark about patriotism, that it is the last refuge of a scoundrel.

As far as the international system is concerned, what are the most striking aspects of the current situation? There is the United Nations sunk in irrelevancy, except as the world's leading humanitarian relief organization. There is a landscape of international relations that seems far more to resemble the bellicose world of pre-1914 Europe than the interdependent, responsible world imagined by the framers of the UN Charter. There is an entire continent, sub-Saharan Africa, mired in an economic calamity largely not of its own making. There is a Europe that pays lip service to human rights, but remains intransigent where its own real interests—such as farm subsidies that effectively condemn sub-Saharan Africa to grinding poverty by limiting its agricultural exports—are concerned. And then there is the United States, seemingly bent on empire.

What was the good news again? That Augusto Pinochet was briefly detained in London, or that Slobodan Milosevic will likely spend the rest of his life in a UN jail? This, while somewhere between two and four million Congolese die in the first general war in Africa since decolonization? The truth is that, outside the developed countries, much of the world is actually in worse shape than it was just a few decades ago. Where there has been progress, if that term is even appropriate in so apocalyptic a context, it has been in the realm of norms—that is, the laws that nations try to evade and ignore, and in which many of the most decent people on this slaughterhouse of a planet continue to believe. But we are deep in loaves-and-fishes land here. To believe that states will suddenly come to their senses and behave as responsible members of an "international community," when few states have ever done this, is, indeed, to believe in miracles.

There is unquestionably a globalized world economy, which remains largely dominated by the United States and is administered through central banks, the International Monetary Fund, and the World Bank. But there is no such thing as an international community, at least not one worthy of the name—assuming, that is, we mean a community of shared values and interests, not just shared membership in the United Nations. For that matter, even the old, Cold War–era blocs are disintegrating: The G-77 Chamber Trade Information Network, the major international organization representing the developing world, now has trouble agreeing on anything beyond the most generic recommendations. The run-up to the Iraq war showed the depth of the divisions within the so-called transatlantic family, and equally sharp splits were evident within Europe during the same period. Never mind community; how can there be any international system when what we have actually witnessed in the period since 9/11 has been the steady erosion of the very idea of consensus in international relations?

There can be little doubt, unfortunately, that the United States has played a major role in this decline. Liberals tend to blame the Bush administration for this, but in reality, there is far more continuity between the Clinton and Bush foreign-policy doctrines than Democrats usually like to concede. It was the Clinton administration, after all, that embraced the principle "with partners if we can, alone if we must." Yes, Clinton and his aides did not try to publicly humiliate the United Nations, but there was nothing genuinely multilateral about their approach to stopping the Bosnian war or resolving the Middle East crisis. Indeed, when then–UN Secretary General Boutros Boutros-Ghali did not do what the Clinton people wanted on the Balkans, he was blocked by the United States in his bid for a second term—even though all the other fourteen members of the Security Council at the time wanted to grant him one. While the atmospherics and aesthetics accompanying the use of American power do indeed distinguish the current administration from its predecessor, in substance the Clinton and Bush teams have been remarkably of one mind on issues surrounding the unilateral application of U.S. military might.

None of this is meant to endorse the radical view, exemplified by such figures of the hard left as Noam Chomsky in the United States and Régis Debray in France, that the collapse of the international system is simply the result of the wickedness of U.S. foreign policy. Such an analysis merely turns the official rhetoric of America's inherent goodness on its head: Instead of being the root of all good, America is seen as the root of all evil. It is true that, by opting for the kind of world-defying unilateralism it chose in Iraq, the United States did a great deal to turn the United Nations into even more of a hollow shell than it already was. But the fact that the United Nations can be effective only if supported (read: underwritten) by the United States testifies to how little substance that system ever really had.

Besides, open defiance of UN rules is hardly the province of the United States. Few countries are more pro–United Nations than the Netherlands. But no Dutch government would dream of acquiescing in the UN drug authority's demand for a strict prohibitionist and punitive policy toward soft drugs. Obviously, there is a difference between bending the rules about making war and the rules about smoking marijuana, but each reveals in its own way the falsity of the idea that any state is going to subordinate its own interests to those of some fictive international "community." All politics is local—an adage international lawyers and human-rights activists could profit from pondering more seriously and respectfully.

To say this is not to demand that people stop dreaming of a better world. Many of us may still aspire to the idea of global citizenship and long for the day when the words "international community" would not be cause for a bitter smile or a sardonic shrug. But it is important to understand how far we are from that day and to act accordingly.

At present, the mood among those Americans who want to continue to uphold some kind of internationalism has tended more and more toward disappointment and bitter resignation. There is much apprehensive talk about empire, much anxiety about the drift of the country, particularly with regard to civil liberties, much (in my view, grotesquely unwarranted) nostalgia for the Clinton administration, while, simultaneously, the legitimate fear of terrorism continues to haunt people's visions of the future.

Is there a way out of this dilemma, beyond simply taking refuge in local politics? However paradoxical this may seem, it is precisely those committed to struggling for a better world in these dark times who stand most desperately in need of abandoning the fantasy of an idealized, law-based international system. In this sense, the profound disenchantment occasioned by the war in Iraq may actually be an opportunity to rethink realism.

It will not come naturally. In the minds of many, realism is associated with the right, with the crimes of a Henry Kissinger and the brutalities of the current neo-liberal order. Usually, it is conflated with cynicism and resignation. But just as there are many species of idealism—from mindless one-worldism to the Bush administration's gloss on muscular, imperial Wilsonianism—so there are many variants of realism. And surely those are worth exploring when empire is all the rage. A realist of the type I am describing is more likely to oppose an attempt to impose democracy by force of arms than an idealist, for whom, alas, force is almost always appealing if the cause is appealing enough. A realist also might insist that the current patterns of consumption in the world are impossible to sustain. In short, there are any number of issues and causes, from women's health and education to debt relief, that are usually conjugated in the language of idealism, but are actually easier to argue for in the name of realism.

What realism cannot do is offer the same kind of millenarian hope that is the essential DNA of idealism. Realism is fundamentally defensive. If anything, that can often make the realist's activism more, rather than less, intense and committed. But there is no getting around the fact that the assumption underlying every variant of realism is that things will not necessarily get better, and may very well grow worse.

People and nations are not altruism machines—never have been, never will be—and it is about time activists learned to live with this fact rather than endlessly, generation after generation, trying to ignore it or wish it away. To say this is in no way to disparage activists. Without them the world would be even more savage and cruel than it already is. But most people commit their lives to their families and, at most, can be mobilized only occasionally in the name of some ideal. They are quite comfortable seeing themselves as citizens of a specific locality, not as global citizens. The idealist dream—whether it is Christians or Muslims proselytizing among the unbelievers, Che Guevara dreaming of creating what he called, to my ears chillingly, a "New Man," or, perhaps, Paul Wolfowitz imagining that he can democratize the Middle East—is that this can be changed.

In contrast, the realist is anti-utopian, skeptical, and, while in no sense passive, acts from the conviction that while there are many wrongs that do indeed need to be righted, and many causes worth defending, not everything is possible, least of all, to paraphrase the slogan of the anti-globalization movement, "another" world. As the great British scientist J.D. Bernal once wrote, "There are two futures—the future of desire and the future of fate, and man's reason has never learned to separate them." A strange note for a Marxist of Bernal's commitments to strike, perhaps, but a perfect encapsulation of the realist creed.

There is, in truth, much reason to fear for the future. Despite all the new norms, there is no evidence that the influence of morality and virtue in international relations has grown. To the contrary, it seems as if we are once more entering the Hobbesian universe of force from which the United Nations' founders imagined they were shepherding the world away. The Iraq war was rightly seen as the harbinger of this colder world, which is why so many decent people, however much they may prefer to keep this to themselves, have turned away from hope and from the belief in global citizenship.

Is there anything to be done? It seems to me that the environmental movement offers the best model to date of the kind of realism I have been outlining. After all, environmental activism is based on a bedrock of harsh, realist calculation—the perception that humanity's survival depends on fundamental reorderings of the way we live now. The argument at its core is not altruism. To the contrary, the environmental movement insists that while yes, it is fine to "care" about the planet in an idealistic way, and that the world would be a far better place (and we as a species might actually survive into the next centuries living in a sustainable world) if we all could think that way, it is self-interest that demands our commitment.

In principle, there is no reason why these same assumptions cannot be exported to the realm of international relations. Admittedly, it is a thin reed on which to base one's hopes. But at this point, it may well be all we have.

Part Two

THE IRAQ WAR AND ITS AFTERMATH

THE LIVES THEY LIVED: COLLATERAL DAMAGE

ON AUGUST 19, A TRUCK BOMB LOADED WITH more than 1,500 pounds of explosives detonated next to the Canal Hotel in Baghdad, right under the offices of Sergio Vieira de Mello, the special envoy of the United Nations to Iraq, killing Vieira de Mello and twenty-one others. For the United Nations, the attack, and specifically the death of Vieira de Mello, was a crippling blow, comparable in its effect on the UN's sense of its own possibility to the impact President Kennedy's murder had on the self-confidence of the United States.

The stature of the United Nations had already been badly damaged by the decision of the United States and its allies to go to war in Iraq in the spring of 2003 without UN authorization. Outside the world body, many had questioned the UN's relevance, and some wondered whether it had any future at all. By sending Vieira de Mello to Iraq after the fall of Baghdad, Secretary General Kofi Annan was trying to reassert the UN's centrality. For if anyone could make it relevant again, it was Vieira de Mello. Vieira de Mello was the man his colleagues believed could transform hopeless situations into hopeful ones and negotiate cease-fires at the height of genocidal wars. He was the United Nations' chief civilian representative in Bosnia in 1993 and its humanitarian coordinator in the Great Lakes region of Africa after the Rwandan genocide of 1994. When NATO expelled Serb forces from Kosovo in 1999, it was Vieira de Mello who was given the task of organizing the first transitional structures in what would prove to be an open-ended UN/NATO protectorate in the breakaway Yugoslav province. And after the Indonesian withdrawal from East Timor in 1999, Vieira de Mello was named head of the UN's transitional authority there. He had a seemingly miraculous knack for sitting down with mortal enemies and reconciling their seemingly irreconcilable positions. As one European diplomat put it after his murder, "Sergio was a man who could go into the foulest situation and come out smelling like a rose."

When people tried to account for his success, they tended to talk of his charm, his erudition (he earned a doctorate from the Sorbonne, spoke four languages fluently and read prodigiously), and even of his quite unforgettable good looks. But those who knew him best discerned the steel beneath the charisma, the born diplomat with a daunting work ethic.

Vieira de Mello apparently believed in the United Nations as it saw itself, the UN at its best—poor in resources but rich in dedication; badly served by its member states, above all the most powerful among them, but nonetheless able, against all the odds, to bring savage wars to a speedier end while alleviating the suffering of the innocent victims of these conflicts; and offering hope and a bedrock of humanitarian principle in a world of power politics, ethnic conflict and realpolitik.

When Vieira de Mello was criticized, though, it was for being too much a devotee of realpolitik. There was the charge that his quasi-religious commitment to the UN's institutional survival made him a servant of the great powers despite himself, since the UN is powerless without them. If the UN's viability would be aided by obliging the United States in Congo, NATO in Kosovo, or the coalition in postwar Iraq, Vieira de Mello often calculated those to be bargains worth making.

Shortly before the Iraq crisis began, he was named UN High Commissioner for Human Rights. The human rights job did not particularly suit him, and he was restive in it. But Vieira de Mello also wondered what he could actually accomplish in occupied Iraq, and at first he resisted the posting. But when Secretary-General Annan persisted, Vieira de Mello acquiesced, assembling an extraordinary team of aides. He flew to Baghdad, insisting that he would stay only four months.

He knew that the United Nations had been shaken by the Iraq crisis, but he said he believed it could renew its claim to relevance in Iraq. He must have known that he was faced with making the best of a bad job. And yet he had been in bad situations before and succeeded. As one of his aides in Baghdad put it, "To the last, Sergio was the most optimistic of all of us."

Vieira de Mello played a critical role in winning legitimacy for Iraq's Governing Council, which, for all its faults and limitations, was the one institution in Iraq that mitigated the relationship between occupier and occupied—between the American forces and the Iraqi people. And yet it seems clear that he, like the institution he served, underestimated the degree to which anti-American forces in Iraq viewed the United Nations as little more than a handmaiden to American power.

And there were undeniable problems with the security

arrangements at Vieira de Mello's headquarters; the UN's own investigations later called its security system dysfunctional. But for Vieira de Mello really to have ensured his security would have required him to turn UN headquarters at the Canal Hotel into a fortress, as the American-occupation authorities have done with their headquarters in Saddam Hussein's former Republican Palace. Doing this would have meant cutting UN staff members off from the Iraqis they were there to serve, however, and this Vieira de Mello was never willing to do. He died, you could argue, for his belief in the bedrock principle that the UN had to be open and independent.

The decision to appoint him testified to the unique role Vieira de Mello played within the world organization. After his murder, Secretary-General Annan was asked whether he would soon be sending a new special envoy to Iraq. Annan replied that he would not do so until such a successor had a clear mandate from the Security Council. A reporter pointed out that Vieira de Mello had operated in Iraq without such a mandate and with considerable success.

Annan replied, "I had only one Sergio."

THE SPECTER OF IMPERIALISM

The Marriage of the Human Rights Left and the New Imperialist Right

A SPECTER IS HAUNTING THE HUMAN RIGHTS movement in the United States, the specter of American imperialism. This paraphrase of Marx's famous remark about Europe and Communism is anything but hyperbole. For over the course of the past ten years, it has become increasingly clear that the world that human rights activists had dreamed of during the long, frustrating decades of Cold War—a world of justice and rule of law; what the billionaire activist and patron of and agenda-setter for the human rights movement, George Soros, has called "open societies"—would be no easier to bring into being after the end of the superpower rivalry than it had been in its heyday. Bosnia, Rwanda, Kosovo, Congo, and East Timor all seemed to demonstrate that. Whatever else separated them, they testified to a world in which it was more rather than less difficult to keep the peace and prevent the most terrible atrocities from taking place. The fact that it was now possible to see such horrors broadcast, live and in real time, on television anywhere in the world, only deepened the sense of crisis, particularly among activists.

Whether this was a crisis of reality or a crisis of expectations; a real historical turn for the worse or the tropism of a self-regarding time to see its own horrors as uniquely, well, horrible, is another question. Certainly, there is considerable evidence to suggest that, despite the commonplace, the twentieth century was not uniquely horrible anywhere *except* in Europe (for many people in the poor world, to cite only the most obvious example, the era's great legacy has been not cemeteries but the end of anywhere between fifty and five hundred years of colonial rule). But the perception has been otherwise. This made the discovery that the end of the Cold War had been a mixed blessing, to say the least—again, except in Europe and the former Soviet Union—so shocking. There would be, human rights activists discovered, no new world order in which such admirable, if utopian documents like the United Nations' Universal Declaration of Human Rights, or even the far more modest Genocide Convention, had a snowball's chance in hell of being implemented.

To the contrary, many, though not obviously all parts of the world were trapped in the same Hobbesian realities as they had always been. States, no matter what UN conventions they had signed, still committed genocide when they saw no other way of staying in power (the Hutu regime in Rwanda in 1994), and even democracy, as Fareed Zakaria shrewdly pointed out, did not turn out to have been the same thing as *liberal* democracy (Malaysia, Uzbekistan, Venezuela, etc., etc.). And the UN, that toothless old scold, proved itself in the killing fields of Bosnia and Rwanda to be worse than useless in preventing mass murder. Actually, though hardly exclusively or even principally at fault in these situations, its actions proved to make them a good deal worse, as, at least in the case of Bosnia, the UN's own report on the Srebrenica massacre virtually conceded.

No one, except, perhaps, the very naïve or the very hypocritical, had ever put that much store in the UN. But the world body had been central in one important respect, particularly to human rights activists, in that it had seemed to embody the promise of multilateral responses to crises like those that consumed the Balkans or the Great Lakes region of Africa in the 1990s. But with the failure of UN peacekeeping there, and in the Kosovo case in 1999, the realization that divisions within the Security Council had not disappeared with the end of the Cold War, and for all intents and purposes precluded the UN from fulfilling the primary mission of ensuring peace and security in the world which had been its reason for coming into existence in the first place, activists came to believe more and more that only unilateral responses, or, to use the think tank cliché, coalitions of the willing, could hope to rescue the Kosovars (or Timorese, or, significantly, Iraqis) from their fate at the hands of thugs and tyrants.

Unsurprisingly, along with this embrace of unilateralism came a new respect for the use of military force, particularly American military force. The American human rights movement had cut its teeth on opposition to the Vietnam war, and, even more importantly, the American proxy wars in Central America in the 1980s. Rhetorically, if not necessarily in practice, it had been anti-imperialist. To be sure, its most successful tactic, which Aryeh Neier, Human Rights Watch's animating spirit in its formative period, called shaming, involved embarrassing the U.S. government by revealing some human rights atrocity by a U.S. client—in Guatemala, say—and then calling on the administration of the day to live up to the country's ideals and values. And of course, the American human rights movement collaborated intimately with Washington in its activism within the Soviet empire, where there was an inescapable congruence of interest. Nonetheless, haunted as it was by the experience of seeing the dark side of U.S. military power in Central America, the human rights movement was highly skeptical of its untrammeled use.

Bosnia changed all that, and for honorable reasons. Given the paralysis of the European powers, the fecklessness of the UN, and the fact that, month after month and year after year, the slaughter in the Balkans went on, it was hardly surprising that activists in America came to feel, quite simply, that if the U.S. military was capable of stopping such horror, then it should; full stop. Realists, who believed that the U.S. had no business intervening when, to turn Tony Blair's boastful rationale for the Kosovo war on its head, only values and not interests were at stake, might be appalled. So were "anti-imperialists," at least of the loopy, Noam Chomsky variety. For them, the U.S. was, in the political sense anyway, for all intents and purposes genetically evil. Nothing it could do could ever have decent consequences, and the fact that the Bosnians and Kosovars and Timorese wanted intervention (as, it seems, many Iraqis do today) was of no consequence to these Manichean true believers in America as wicked demiurge.

But the American human rights movement had never been realist or nationalist in either the isolationist sense or in that of John Adams, who had so famously insisted that it was not the duty of the United States to "go out and fight monsters," let alone be prey to the political Lysenkoism of the American hard left. To the contrary, it had, from its inception, been idealist to the core. More than idealist, when all was said and done, it had been Wilsonian.

Contra John Adams, it believed that America's task and sworn duty *was* to right the world's wrongs, to make it "safe for democracy," as Wilson had famously said, and, having made it safe, do everything within its power to see that that democratic ideal took hold in every corner of the globe. The problem for human rights activists, in other words, was not the enormous power of the U.S. in and of itself, but rather the way that power was employed (that is, legally or illegally) and, most important of all, the moral and political uses to which it was put.

It is significant, I think that there is no sustained critique of power *qua* power even in the commonsense terms of Lord Acton's dictum that "power corrupts and absolute power corrupts absolutely," let alone in those of a Michel Foucault, in the U.S. human rights movement. If anything, the reverse is true. No senior figure at George Soros' Open Society Institute seems all that troubled by the undeniable fact that Soros' money, influence, and easy access to those who rule our world, puts him in the paradoxical position of furthering a democratic agenda by undemocratic means; and no one in a leadership position at Human Rights Watch has ever evidenced unease over that organization's ever-increasing reliance on rich individual private donors, notably Soros himself, and major international corporations, like the London-based Tetra Laval. And it is hardly surprising that they don't. For the vision of the American human rights movement, like that of Woodrow Wilson, has been and remains fundamentally Platonic in the most undemocratic sense of the term—a caste of Platonic Guardians seeing to the best interests of the population at large, and accountable, in the final analysis, only to itself.

In a sense, what happened in the 1990s was that the American human rights movement simply moved, at least partially, from a

Wilsonianism of moral suasion and law-based regimes to a Wilsonianism dependent on the use of military force, above all, American military force. In fairness, this was as much the product of despair as of any change in convictions. UN peacekeeping demonstrably failed in the 1990s; it was a broken instrument, and one that was highly unlikely to be repaired, no matter how many commissions bursting with eminent international persons set their much revered minds to coming up with alternatives they themselves, in their less grandiose moments, had no chance of implementing. And international law, despite the advent of what, for activists, were the pathbreaking events of the ad hoc tribunals for the former Yugoslavia and for Rwanda, the Mine Ban Treaty, and the fledgling International Criminal Court, was, to put it charitably, a work in progress. No one seriously expected these instruments to prevent the next Rwanda.

But then what was to be done? The answer, for many at least, was to harness American military power, power the likes of which the world had never seen, to this noble cause of protecting the victims of genocide and mass slaughter, securing people's liberties, and spreading—call it what you will—open societies, democracy, liberal capitalism. For once one has accepted the premise that military power has to be used, there is no real alternative to U.S. military power. On a moral level, what are the alternatives? Russia or China, the only two other states with the capacity to airlift large numbers of troops to some remote conflict zone and keep them supplied? The brain rebels. As for Europe, it has chosen to be militarily weak—chosen, not been forced as Robert Kagan wrongly asserts in his vastly over-estimated recent book, *Of Paradise and Power,* since when Europe opts for technological competition with the U.S. as the experience of Airbus eclipsing Boeing as the world's preeminent supplier of commercial aircraft demonstrates. But by making this choice, Europe has for all intents and purposes removed itself from serious consideration as an alternative to U.S. power. A Europe with Germany at its center, pacifist Germany whose deepest ambition seems to be a gigantic Switzerland, may do no harm, but is unlikely to have much of a role except, like Switzerland itself, in the 'humanitarian' aftermaths of wars.

And so, for lack of a better choice, activists made their historic compromise with realities of U.S. power. In her book, *A Problem from Hell,* which in many ways is a breviary for this new military humanism (the phrase is Chomsky's; his ability to coin good titles is as great as his inability to think with any form of nuance), Samantha Power laments that "the forward looking, consoling refrain of 'never again,' a testament to America's can-do spirit, never grappled with the fact that the country had done nothing, practically or politically, to prepare itself to respond to genocide." [p. xxi] The theme of the book, Wilsonian to the core, is that, thanks to its vast power, the United States can prevent or curb genocide if it chooses to. For power, the scandal of U.S. policy throughout the twentieth century, which she delineates with great finesse, is that it has not chosen such a course. But Power is not in mourning. Like many activists, her book is a call to arms—in the instance, quite literally, for she means American arms. She ends with a famous remark by George Bernard Shaw, much loved by activists of all stripes, to the effect that the reasonable man adapts himself to the world. The unreasonable one persists in trying to adapt the world to himself. Therefore, all progress depends on the unreasonable man. And she concludes, "After a century of doing so little to prevent, suppress, and punish genocide, Americans must join and thereby legitimate the ranks of the unreasonable."

The unreasonable? It sounds stirring, but what exactly does it mean? For Power, it obviously cannot mean Benito Mussolini or Stalin, two "unreasonable" men for whom Shaw expressed some considerable sympathy in his lifetime. And yet while Power clearly means *her (our?)* sort of unreasonable people—those who are wracked by conscience, who seek a better world, who cannot bear to stand idly by while terrible things are done that their government had the means if not the will to prevent—the fact that she could conclude her book with what, in effect, amounts to a blank check for action offers an insight into the millenarian tenor of interventionist human rights activism. She might, with equal rhetorical flourish, have lectured her fellow citizens with the old Black Power saying that "if you're not part of the solution, you're part of the problem"—another slogan that neither answers the most essential questions—above all about the responsibility one has in advocating war when one will have little or no responsibility or say in how it is waged—nor is, when you think about it, all that, well, true.

Like many human rights activists, however, Power is contemptuous of caution. She borrows Albert O. Hirschmann's categories of futility, perversity, and jeopardy to lambaste those who oppose what she describes as "progressive reform" on the grounds of its unintended consequences. "Officials and citizens who oppose action," she writes, "provide detailed accounts of all that can go wrong but rarely admit the possibility of success, of *desirable* unintended consequences, or of some negative consequences but an overall net positive gain."

In these sentences, Power sounds like no one so much as Donald Rumsfeld or Paul Wolfowitz defending the U.S. attack on Iraq against doubters and naysayers. Indeed, this faith in desirable unintended consequences has been at the heart of the Bush administration's position all along. They insist that the U.S. is going to war because of the threat of Iraqi weapons and its violation of relevant UN resolutions, but add that the overthrow of one of the worst tyrants on the planet may, yes, have all sorts of positive effects on the region, and, in any case will be, just as Power puts it, a net positive gain.

Like a number of other human rights activists, Power has recently expressed misgivings about the war in Iraq. But her opposition is not to an attack on Iraq, but the way the Bush administration envisages it. In a recent article in *The New Republic,* she reproached the Bush administration for its tone, for its refusal to acknowledge America's past sins, and above all, for its inconsistency, and what she called its *"a la cartism."* Reading these paragraphs, one imagines Power may be having second thoughts about the war itself, but in reality her reservations are only about the way the Bush administration went about it. "Liberals and conservatives, hawks and doves alike, must see that American power *can* [italics in original] be a force for human rights around the world, *and* greater human rights enjoyment is an indispensable requirement for the preservation of human rights."

Power could not be clearer. For her, at least potentially, human rights is the moral warrant power and American power the guarantor of human rights throughout the world. The old imperialists of the Teddy Roosevelt era could scarcely have said it better. Interestingly, T. R. is a hero of Power's book for his demand that the architects of the Armenian genocide be brought to account after World War I, and his belief that no peace deal should have been signed by the U.S. with Turkey until they were. So once more, Power finds herself in unexpected company. For if any figure from the past is admired by the principal figures within the Bush administration and their conservative and neoconservative allies, it is the first President Roosevelt. For them, he incarnates the proper mix of power and idealism, the empire-builder and the righter of wrongs.

Power is anything but unique, except in the admirable sense that she has made the case for legal imperialism more elegantly and fastidiously than any other advocate on the American scene today. But she is also emblematic of the historic compromise between the human rights movement and the American empire that has been taking place for some time in the United States. This approach, though often expressed more judiciously and with less passion, can be encountered almost anywhere one cares to look in the human rights movement these days. Power's Harvard colleague, Michael Ignatieff, has argued that, at least in rogue states like Iraq, failed states like Somalia or the former Yugoslavia, or helpless states like Haiti, the U.S. is "the last hope for democracy and stability." He may be right, of course, but is saying this sufficient? Is it really the duty of the U.S. to go out and fight monsters? Both Power and Ignatieff seem to think it is. In Power's case, more consistency and less *a la cartism* would almost inevitably lead to endless wars of altruism—one, two, three, many Kosovos, to paraphrase Che Guevara. Are there really limits, or, to put it another way, is there really no hubris the American human rights movement is not glad to be guilty of?

In a sense, Iraq remains a special case. Mainstream human rights groups like Human Rights Watch have long seen it as guilty of genocide and tried, as Power narrates in her book, to get Saddam Hussein brought before some international court. Power concludes her chapter on Iraq by remarking bitterly that, "to this day, however, no Iraqi soldier or political leader has been punished for atrocities committed against the Kurds." But how was that punishment to be meted out? At times, human rights activists seem to behave as if one can have Nuremberg-style justice without a Nuremberg-style military occupation of the countries where the war criminals live. In reality, however, the choice is stark: These human rights regimes will be imposed by force of arms or they will not be imposed at all, and it is disingenuous of a human rights movement that, wittingly or unwittingly over the course of the 1990s, set the moral table for the new imperial mood in America, to suddenly recoil from the Bush administration Captain Reynault–style because, shock, horror, they're unilateralist, Bible-thumping, gun-loving, anti-civil liberties reactionaries.

Who is kidding whom? The logic of human rights activism, from Rwanda to the Balkans, and from East Timor to Burma, has been interventionist to the core. But it has been interventionist with a vestigial bad conscience. Human rights activists want UN sanctions, want the United States to talk the talk of multilateralism, or, as Power puts it, to understand that "tone matters." Tone, not substance. This is the imperial vocation as refracted through Lewis Carroll. Indeed, for activists to now, after a decade of calling for the U.S. to unleash its power, lament the demise of multilateralism and regimes of international law is grotesque and unseemly. What did the Human Rights Watch officials and Soros Foundation officials and the rest think that they were doing? How could Human Rights Watch call for Saddam Hussein to be brought to justice (and what did it imagine the mechanism for this would be, moral suasion?) and now oppose the war in Iraq in a credible manner.

In the end, it is difficult to escape the thought that the real objections of human rights activists are aesthetic rather than political. Would they have felt the same way had Bill Clinton been in power? I doubt it. It is loathsome to think that we are really back in the realm of old bicoastal snobberies, and that this bane and disgrace of American liberalism, with its deep-seated feeling that Bush, Ashcroft, Rumsfeld, are not "our" sort of people, has simply reemerged. Above all, if it is true, as Perry Anderson has asserted, that Clinton would have waged the same war and been supported, then the late opposition among human rights activists to the administration's war plans cannot be taken at face value. It is not a quarrel between imperialists and anti-imperialists but among imperialists—a textbook case of the narcissism of small differences of which Michael Ignatieff reminded us, in a different context, some years ago.

And in the battle (if one can call it that) between imperialists, it is surely the real ones, that is, the conservatives, who seem more focused and clear-headed. They, at least, are willing to state clearly what they are for. For them, Benjamin Franklin's remark that "America's cause was the cause of all mankind" is simply an article of faith. Everything proceeds from this confident belief. If, in America today, the old argument between John Adams and Franklin seems to have swung decidedly in favor of Franklin, and we are, in a sense, all Wilsonians now. But if the choice is between what the conservative writer Max Boot has called the "hard Wilsonianism" of (when all else fails) unilateral U.S. action and the "soft Wilsonianism" of the UN Security Council and international legal regimes, then the events of the past ten years have already shown clearly which argument was going to win, and will continue to win. It is like a choice between a *faux* conservative and a real one: the real one wins every time, and with good reason.

Whose Teddy Roosevelt is more persuasive—Power's denationalized, depoliticized legalist celebrity calling for an end to impunity, or Max Boot's imperialist? There is simply no contest. In any case, having castigated the UN in the Balkans (during the siege of Sarajevo, George Soros accused the organization of serving as a guard in a concentration camp), and pressed for evading the UN Security Council over Kosovo, it is difficult to see how human rights activists and their sympathizers can get on their high legalist horses now. They will of course argue that U.S. intervention in Iraq is not disinterested. But succor alone can never be the purpose of empire; it can at best be its by-product; and it is useless to pretend otherwise. Again, this is why the imperial dreams of American neoconservatives like Boot or Kagan make so much more sense than the vacillations of the humanitarian left, which, at its worst, has found it easier to support U.S. military intervention when there were no U.S. interests at stake than to support a venture along the Euphrates that is, indeed, a mix of values and interests.

The real lesson is that human rights—the secular religion of the West, as Michael Ignatieff and others have rightly called it—cannot provide any serious opposition to the American empire because human rights has become, however inconsistently applied, the official ideology of the American empire—something conservatives have understood, even if most activists themselves have not. Both might concede that they are on a millenarian kick, seeking to bring justice to the world. But what activists have failed to take in is that while they may differ radically with the Bush administration on matters of domestic policy (there is certainly no confluence of either interests or values there!), and decry the administration's style, in substantive terms, in matters like the Balkans, Rwanda, and, yes, Iraq, they are on the *same* millenarian kick as the administration. Both believe American nonintervention has made the world a far crueler place; both believe it is time to intervene; what they differ about, in short, are the atmospherics that should accompany the intervention.

The ghost at the banquet of the American experiment has always been the ghost of empire. Now it seems that if a conservative administration and its improbable allies on the humanitarian left have their way, the only remaining question will be what sort of empire. Will it be American only, or, as seems probable, will the United Nations' *next* humiliation be to serve as a sort of colonial office to U.S. power? And these are not easy questions. One may prefer the American republic to the American empire that appears to be in the process of being born, with George Bush as our Octavian, but is there a choice?

Given the extent to which I have campaigned for certain military interventions, above all in the Balkans and the Great Lakes region of Africa, it would be disingenuous to pretend that my views have not changed since then. They have. Emphatically. I would still claim a certain degree of consistency in the sense that I never supported *humanitarian* intervention in Bosnia. What I campaigned for was a political intervention based not on humanitarian norms but on ideological affinity. I believed that the U.S. should support the fledgling democracy of Bosnia-Herzegovina against the nationalists and fascists bent on destroying it. But I never believed it was possible for the U.S. (or the UN or the European Union for that matter; these millenarian dreams have a resonance far beyond America's shores) to create a democracy out of whole cloth—as we will have to do in Iraq if we are to be successful there. I have changed my mind in the sense that I did not imagine Bosnia, or, had it happened, Rwanda, would become a template for the messianic dream of remaking the world in either the image of American democracy or of the legal utopias of international human rights law. In other words, I imagined they would be exceptional acts, not the routine business of a hubristic altruism, maddened by a strange mix of ethical compulsion and national pride, and nourished by an overconfidence—that we will be successful in the first place, that we will know what to do with our success, that, unlike every empire that has preceded us, we will not be corrupted by that success—that is breath-taking even in a nation so wedded to self-confidence as the United States of America.

AFTERTHOUGHT

Obviously, I am not arguing that human rights activists, relief workers, or committed writers like Samantha Power endorsed the war in Iraq. Most did not. But this essay does argue that the logic of the argument for intervention on human rights and humanitarian grounds is an argument for the de facto selective recolonization of the world and that neoconservatives are on solid ground when they insist that it is they and not the human rights activists who espouse the more consistent position when they favor interventions in Bosnia, Rwanda, Kosovo, and *Iraq. Again, this is what I myself argued for in "A New Age of Liberal Imperialism," and I believe that even changing sides has not blinded me to the force of this position. The fact that many of those who opposed the deployment of U.S. troops to overthrow Saddam Hussein were soon calling for what would have amounted to an invasion of Darfur on humanitarian grounds seems to me to exemplify the dilemma human rights interventionists face. In fairness, it is a dilemma all of us face when we think about war.*

END OF EMPIRE

THESE DAYS, EVEN THE STAUNCHEST ADVOCATES of the Bush administration's plan to overthrow Saddam Hussein and remake Iraq are hard-pressed to square their predictions about how things would turn out with what has actually happened—and failed to happen—on the ground. Saddam Hussein had no nuclear arsenal; Iraqi oil revenues were insufficient to cover even a fraction of the cost of the reconstruction; U.S. troops have earned the enmity of many of the Iraqis who had supported the invasion; and far from becoming a bastion of U.S.–style democracy, Iraq's future is likely to be determined by a Shiite religious hierarchy that has little sympathy for any meaningful separation of church and state. Thus do neoconservative dreams turn to dust in Iraq.

Dreams, it has turned out, cannot always be converted into realities, no matter how smart, determined, and powerful you are. In a country that uses the phrase "American Dream" proudly and without irony, this sobering thought may not gain much traction in normal times. But these are not normal times, and as a triumphal military campaign to overthrow Saddam has turned into a bitter and seemingly inconclusive occupation, many Americans who supported the war have begun to realize that they were misled. The vision of a Middle East recast in America's image has turned out to be wishful thinking. And instead of being the first step in a long campaign of regional social engineering at the point of an M-16, Iraq appears more likely to be an exception than a rule. The American public may give its leaders the benefit of the doubt during wartime, but sooner or later a healthy skepticism returns, no matter how much an administration keeps fostering a sense of national emergency.

The war came about because of a perfect storm, a confluence between forces that included: neoconservatives bent on transforming the Middle East; old-fashioned American nationalists like Donald Rumsfeld whose nineteenth-century model, suitably updated, was the expeditionary war against the Barbary pirates (a matter of sending out the troops to kill the republic's enemies and then bringing them home); those who believed that America looked weak after 9/11 and that someone had to be made an example of; those for whom reliance on Saudi oil had become too dangerous and Iraq beckoned as an alternative; and, finally, a Congress traumatized by 9/11 and deprived of almost all will to resist the administration. It is a convergence unlikely to be repeated for a very long time.

The war on terrorism makes sense to Americans because they view it, legitimately, as a war of self-defense. But Iraq seems less and less like such a war. Instead, it seems more and more like a foreign adventure, fought for reasons other than the ones cited by the Bush administration. The disappointing course of the occupation may well have discredited the more flamboyant claims of the war's neoconservative supporters, and, as a result, immunized the public against further adventures of this type for the foreseeable future. No matter what the Coalition Provisional Authority and the Pentagon may say, the public senses that the occupation of Iraq demonstrates the limitations—rather than the potential—of military power.

ALL GOVERNMENTS lie to their people; what is remarkable, and worrying, is the extent to which officials in Washington, and their emissaries in Baghdad, appear to be lying to themselves. To people who spend more time with Iraqis than with Americans, the U.S. occupation headquarters in Baghdad can often seem like an alternate universe. It is full of purposeful, dedicated, astonishingly driven and hardworking people whose account of what is taking place in the country simply does not seem to coincide with what most of us see every day. And the longer one stays in Iraq—I have spent more than four months there since the fall of Baghdad—the more puzzling and self-destructive the administration's stance comes to appear. To hear U.S. officials in Baghdad tell it, for example, anti–U.S. feeling in Iraq is limited to a small minority of Iraqis. In fact, of course, many of the overwhelming majority of Iraqis who welcomed the U.S. invasion now despise the U.S. occupation—a perfectly reasonable distinction that nonetheless seems to be lost on both supporters and opponents of U.S. policy in Iraq.

It would be comforting to believe that this blindness is simply due to the extent to which U.S. officials, largely for security reasons, are cut off from ordinary Iraqis. But the problem goes far deeper than that. Again and again, while talking to U.S. officials both in Iraq and Washington, I have had the sense that their confidence in the mission was less a matter of reasoned judgment than of faith.

The mindset is one of having a virtual monopoly on truth. The United States is the benign hegemon. It alone has truly understood the challenge posed by terrorists and rogue states and has taken the necessary measures to combat this threat. Those who do not share this assessment are either cowards, appeasers, or useful idiots of the terrorists.

There is something quasi-religious about this worldview, something eerily reminiscent of the old Protestant notion of the Elect of God, privileged, or perhaps burdened, by knowledge and responsibilities others have been spared. To those convinced of their own rectitude, convinced that the fate of the world depends on their ability to act, the details of making the case that Saddam Hussein had weapons of mass destruction seem to have appeared almost trivial. No wonder one former U.S. intelligence analyst referred to the administration's penchant for "faith-based intelligence."

This combination of the intellectual's belief in the power of ideas and the nationalist's belief in American exceptionalism is what marked the neoconservative movement from its beginnings—and what made it so appealing to the Bush administration. In 2000, candidate Bush had argued against expanding U.S. commitments abroad, had derided the Clinton administration's nation-building efforts in the Balkans, and had cast a skeptical eye on what he saw as excessive U.S. involvement in the Middle East peace process. But after 9/11, the administration needed a set of ideas to underpin its response to the terrorist attacks—in other words, an ideology. The neoconservatives' "philosophical warfare," with its good-versus-evil typology, fit the bill perfectly.

Now, though, the neoconservatives are no longer in the ascendant. Right-wing think tanks like the American Enterprise Institute and the Project for the New American Century might continue to carry the torch for the grand project of remaking the Islamic Middle East, but in political terms it has become clear that this is a nonstarter. Public-opinion polls demonstrate that there is very limited support for further military adventures in the Middle East (except in cases of a specific perceived threat). Having succeeded in many ways, the neoconservative movement has clearly failed to build a broad-based domestic constituency for its views. It remains what it always was, a largely inside-the-Beltway phenomenon.

And even in Washington policy circles, the neoconservatives' vision—and especially their reliance on military force as the key instrument in U.S. foreign policy—has lost support. Some hawks within the administration now concede that between Afghanistan, Iraq, and the Korean peninsula, the U.S. military is stretched to the breaking point, with "Ten Army divisions doing twelve divisions' work," as Senator John McCain has put it. Even before the war, many American senior officers had grave reservations about the wisdom of preemptive, unilateral war: "Colin Powell is my secretary of defense, not those neocons," was the way one midgrade officer put it to me in February of 2003. The fact that, by the time the current troop rotation is completed, nearly 40 percent of U.S. forces on the ground in Iraq will come from the National Guard and Reserves tells you all you need to know about how little appetite there is in Washington for continued aggressive military action in Iraq.

OF COURSE, it is conceivable that after the election, if Bush wins, the pendulum will swing back once more. The neoconservatives may be in retreat, but some of the most significant impulses they represent did not originate with them and will not disappear with them; a version of those impulses dates back to the founding of the republic. (It was Benjamin Franklin who wrote that America's cause "is the cause of all mankind"; it was Robert Kagan who recently claimed that the United States must act "in ways that benefit all humanity or, at the very least, the part of humanity that shares its liberal principles.")

But at its inception, and through most of U.S. history, the mainstream interpretation of the American revolutionary project was that it was about serving as an example—"the shining city on the hill"—and not about remaking the world in its image by force of arms. Spreading democracy by military means was the historical ambition of that other revolutionary Western democracy, France. It is ironic that the same neoconservatives who despise the French more than perhaps any other people are far closer to the armies of Robespierre or Napoleon in their approach to spreading "the idea of freedom" (the phrase is Douglas Feith's) than they are to Washington, Jefferson, or Adams.

The change in the American understanding of the fundamental purpose of foreign wars—a change that Woodrow Wilson began with his "war to end all wars"—became institutionalized during World War II and the Cold War. These were wars as zero-sum games, with no outcome viewed as acceptable, morally licit even, except total victory. Whether it was Roosevelt demanding the unconditional surrender of Germany and Japan, Kennedy promising that the United States would "pay any price, bear any burden" to defend liberty (an astonishing claim when you think about it: any price? any burden?), or Reagan describing the Soviet Union as an "evil empire," the conflict was one between good and evil. The only administrations to almost completely buck this apocalyptic trend were those of Richard Nixon and, to some extent, George Herbert Walker Bush.

Still, the current neoconservative vision is very different in scope, and to some degree in substance, from traditional American exceptionalism. In particular, its faith in unilateral military action goes very much against the American grain. Not only have Americans generally regarded foreign adventures with skepticism, but the strategy of going it alone has rarely been popular over the long term—particularly when it attracts criticisms from America's closest allies. That is why British participation in the overthrow of Saddam Hussein, useful though dispensable in military terms, was indispensable in political terms. And the fact that it would be impossible for Tony Blair to join a U.S. attack on Syria, let alone Iran, is not the least of the impediments to such future campaigns.

Proponents of an imperial America may view domestic policy as a distraction (writing in the *New Republic,* one conservative pundit said he supported Senator Lieberman for president and didn't much care about the senator's domestic record). But for the public, foreign intervention comes second to the nation's needs at home. They need to be persuaded that a war is necessary for their own well-being. What has happened since the fall of Baghdad is that this claim, always debatable, has come to many to seem false.

Of course the United States will act in its own interest and will usually do what it can get away with doing. But self-interest would seem to demand that any U.S. administration not act in ways that deepen anti-American feeling, serve as a recruiting slogan for the Osama bin Ladens of this world, exacerbate tensions with many of America's principal trading partners, and distract the administration's attention from crises that are either more important

(Korea) or closer to home (Haiti, Mexico, Colombia). Events on the ground in Iraq every day, from attacks on U.S. forces to the Shiite mobilization, demonstrate that the administration overestimated the transformative power of military action; the burgeoning deficit suggests that this was a war the United States could ill afford. It was this due diligence that the neoconservative theorists of the war never carried out.

The United States has so much power that, barring a miracle, it is difficult to see how the temptation to use it unwisely will ever disappear. But there is a profound difference between a temptation and a fait accompli. The license of the powerful—and it is a terrible license—can be exercised or not exercised. That, in a democracy, is a political choice. The failure of the neoconservative vision for Iraq has created an opening for debating this choice by bringing under scrutiny—for the first time since 9/11—the set of assumptions that presents the United States as a revolutionary power whose destiny it is to lead the world toward the promised land by force of arms.

With the doctrine of preemptive war, the Bush administration went far beyond the utopian credos of America's founders—or even of Wilson, Roosevelt, and Reagan. It is, fundamentally, a doctrine of endless war. Only the organizational skills and ideological determination of the neoconservatives and the trauma of 9/11 obscured that fact for a time. But as the reality of what occupying Iraq has really involved sinks in, it is doubtful such a doctrine can be maintained. And in a time when there is not much good news, that is very good news indeed.

THE WAY WE LIVE NOW

A Notion of War

IN WASHINGTON, IT IS OFTEN ASSUMED THAT the answer to every crisis is to be found in a Big Idea—"the vision thing," as President George Herbert Walker Bush once called it, somewhat dismissively. Just as nature abhors a vacuum, so administrations abhor an absence of ideas (or at least convenient catch phrases). Muddling through, which is the reality of politics, rarely seems enough.

Nowhere has this been more true than in the realm of foreign policy. Iraq has been the perfect example. President George H. W. Bush's big idea about Iraq, rolling back Saddam Hussein, gave way to President Clinton's big idea about Iraq, containment, which gave way to President George W. Bush's big idea about Iraq, Iraqi liberation. But as events have shown, the liberation of Iraq alone hasn't solved the problems there, so as is often the case in Washington, one reigning idea has gradually transformed into another reigning big idea: Iraqification, the notion that what is needed to improve the situation there (and bring American troops home) is a quick transfer of control over security and the political process to the Iraqis.

For many Americans old enough to remember the Vietnam War, the term Iraqification carries the same baggage of defeat and withdrawal that Vietnamization did a generation ago. For others, it simply seems like a sensible response to the difficulties the United States has encountered in Iraq in the aftermath of the ousting of Saddam Hussein—a sensible midterm correction or readjustment of America's original postwar plan. Still others, notably within the Bush administration, insist that Iraqification was at the heart of the U.S. government's planning for a postwar Iraq from the start, even if the public emphasis had been elsewhere.

But if opinions are mixed about what, if anything, the recent enthusiasm in Washington for Iraqification tells us about America's success or failure in Iraq, there is little question that it has become the reigning idea about how Iraq's future will be organized. It is an idea, however, with a contradiction at its core.

The problem is less that different people use Iraqification to pass different judgments on the war but that the idea means so many different things to so many different people. In this way it is again like a lot of big ideas in Washington—a term everyone uses while obscuring different, even antithetical approaches. Here are some possibilities for what Iraqification might look like. While it is impossible to say which will eventually prevail, each of them can be supported by trends and facts on the ground in Iraq today.

According to the gloomiest of these possibilities, Iraqification does play out like Vietnamization. The U.S. raises an Iraqi army, but that army has no real legitimacy among the Iraqi people as a whole (raising an army before establishing a political structure that can command its loyalty is always risky). As a result, Iraqification fails to quell the guerrilla insurgency under way in Baghdad, the so-called Sunni Triangle, and the northern city of Mosul, and the U.S. is faced with the choice of either withdrawing, presumably on domestic political grounds, or committing huge new forces to what would in effect be the second part of the war.

Another version of Iraqification involves cutting a deal with some senior Iraqi official from the Saddam Hussein era and allowing him to rule—a "housebroken Saddam" in the words of the Cato Institute's Ted Galen Carpenter. This idea is by no means completely fanciful. Before the war, some administration officials hinted that if Saddam Hussein gave up power, this would satisfy Washington's desire for regime change. Presumably, such a figure would be able to quell the uprising in the Sunni Triangle.

An equally defeatist but perhaps less morally unpalatable Iraqification, one that involves Iraqification through abolition, was most recently suggested by a former president of the Council on Foreign Relations, Leslie Gelb. It calls for the partition of Iraq into three states—one Kurdish, one Sunni, and one Shiite. With each major constituent group in Iraq having its own state, fighting would presumably cease and the United States could exit from Iraq with its own security concerns met and a relatively stable situation on the ground.

Another version of Iraqification being considered in Washington is for the U.S. to come to some sort of understanding with the Shiite hierarchy and effectively concede that not only would the Shiites dominate a post–Saddam-Hussein Iraq—something that is probably inevitable anyway given the fact that they make up about 60 percent of the population and that 15 percent or so more live in a semiautonomous Kurdistan—but also that Iraq's destiny is to become a moderate theocracy; in other words, not Iran under Khomeini, but not Turkey either.

Finally, there is the option that most Iraqi exiles, many people in the Bush administration (particularly the neoconservatives), and certainly many Iraqis hoped for: that Iraqification will actually mean the installation not just of representative democracy in Iraq (the Shiite state option does this as well), but also of a genuinely pluralistic and nontheological state. The rights of religious and ethnic minorities (including secular people) would be respected, and women would be free not to submit to the dictates of religious authorities. In other words, an Iraq that, if it does not exactly become the Czech Republic, does allow its citizens at least as many freedoms as those enjoyed by people in Lebanon or Turkey.

These variants of Iraqification may indeed be incompatible in theory. In practice, of course, big ideas in Washington often evolve so fast that their real role is to convince the public that something is being done to address a problem—until the next big idea comes along, that is.

WERE SANCTIONS RIGHT?

As the war in Iraq recedes, the challenges of occupying and rebuilding the country seem to grow more daunting with every passing day. It is becoming clear, though, that Iraq's devastation is not primarily the result of American bombing during the war or of the looting that followed it, but of the economic crisis that befell the country before the first shot was fired. There is still little consensus about what happened in Iraq during the years before the war or who is to blame. But the quest for answers has reawakened a fierce and bitter controversy over Iraq policy in the 1990s.

For officials in Washington and London and for American administrators now in Iraq, that country's postwar woes are essentially the legacy of Saddam Hussein's tyrannical, cruel, and corrupt rule. As L. Paul Bremer III, the civilian administrator of postwar Iraq, recently said of Hussein, "While his people were starving—literally, in many cases, starving—while he was killing tens of thousands of people, Saddam and his cronies were taking money, stealing it, really, from the Iraqi people."

But others argue that the fundamental reason Iraq is in such terrible shape is not Hussein's brutality but rather the comprehensive regime of economic sanctions that the United Nations Security Council imposed on Iraq for almost thirteen years, sharply restricting all foreign trade. It was these sanctions, they claim, that brought this once rich country to its knees.

For many people, the sanctions on Iraq were one of the decade's great crimes, as appalling as Bosnia or Rwanda. Anger at the United States and Britain, the two principal architects of the policy, often ran white hot. Denis J. Halliday, the United Nations humanitarian coordinator in Iraq for part of the sanctions era, expressed a widely held belief when he said in 1998: "We are in the process of destroying an entire society. It is as simple and terrifying as that." Even today, Clinton-era American officials ranging from Madeleine K. Albright, the former secretary of state, and James P. Rubin, State Department spokesman under Albright, to Nancy E. Soderberg, then with the National Security Council, speak with anger and bitterness over the fervor of the antisanctions camp. As Soderberg put it to me, "I could not give a speech anywhere in the U.S. without someone getting up and accusing me of being responsible for the deaths of 500,000 Iraqi children."

The end of the war has at last made it possible to find out what the effects of sanctions on Iraq really were. American officials from the administrations of George Bush Sr. and Bill Clinton are now willing to speak candidly about the human costs of sanctions, and Iraqis are also able to speak far more openly than they were before Saddam Hussein's ouster.

Many of the diplomats who constructed and administered the sanctions policy still defend them steadfastly. Richard Holbrooke, who served as ambassador to the United Nations under President Clinton, says, "The concept of sanctions is not just still valid; it's necessary. What else fills in the gap between pounding your breast and indulging in empty rhetoric and going to war besides economic sanctions?"

Albright insists that sanctions cannot be ruled out in the future when formulating policy, whether in Washington or at the Security Council, for dealing with such tyrannies as North Korea, Zimbabwe, or Myanmar, formerly Burma.

And James Rubin asks, "What should we have done, just lift sanctions and hope for the best? I believed then and believe now that that was just too risky, given Saddam Hussein's past, his repeated attempts to invade his neighbors, his treatment of his own people and the weapons we knew he was developing."

According to Rubin, sanctions were the sole available choice that did not imply allowing Saddam Hussein to do what he pleased in the region. And officials of the first President Bush's administration, hardly known for endorsing many of the policies later formulated by Clinton's foreign-policy team, broadly agree. "What we were trying to do by putting sanctions in was to prevent Hussein from threatening the region," recalled General Brent Scowcroft, the national security adviser for the first President Bush. "They worked in the sense that he was never able to rebuild his conventional army. When this war started, the Iraqi Army had no more than one-third of the strength it had possessed at the beginning of the first gulf war. But imagine that there had been no sanctions. Is it reasonable to suppose that the weakened Iraqi Army we just faced would have been so weak? I doubt it."

These observations do not answer the question of whether any policy, no matter how strategically sound, is worth the deaths of 500,000 Iraqi children—a figure that originated in a UNICEF report on infant mortality in sanctions-era Iraq and became the rallying cry of antisanctions campaigners. And the argument against sanctions on Iraq went beyond even this single, horrifying statistic. Sanctions, their opponents insist, transformed a country that in the 1980s was the envy of the developing world in terms of investments in health, education, and physical infrastructure into a place where everyone (except the half-million or so members of Saddam Hussein's Baath Party and their families and cronies) was dependent on United Nations food aid, where infant mortality rates had skyrocketed, educational outcomes had collapsed, and diseases that had disappeared were reappearing, sometimes at epidemic levels.

American officials may quarrel with the numbers, but there is little doubt that at least several hundred thousand children who could reasonably have been expected to live died before their fifth birthdays. The damage, according to those who fought against sanctions, was terrible, medieval. It was, in the literal sense, unconscionable, since those who died had not themselves developed weapons of mass destruction or invaded Kuwait. Rather, they were the cannon fodder for Hussein's war and the victims of his repression.

Madeleine Albright was widely excoriated in 1996 for telling a television interviewer who asked her about the deaths of Iraqi children caused by sanctions, "This is a very hard choice, but the price, we think the price is worth it."

She says now that she regrets the comment—"It was a genuinely stupid thing to say"—and in a recent interview seemed still to be struggling with the moral and strategic questions that underlie the sanctions debate. For Albright, the comprehensive regime of sanctions imposed on Iraq represented at best a tragic choice between unhappy alternatives—a search for the lesser evil.

As Albright put it to me, "I wish people understood that these are not black and white choices; the choices are really hard." Sanctions like the ones that were imposed on Iraq, she said, "are a blunt instrument. That's their tragedy. What was so terrible for me was that I did see the faces of the people who were suffering—even if I thought then and think now that the sufferings of the Iraqi people were Saddam's doing, not ours. There's a terrible price you pay. A terrible price."

The actual history of American sanctions on Iraq is fairly straightforward. On August 2, 1990, in response to Iraq's invasion and annexation of Kuwait, the United Nations Security Council passed Resolution 661, imposing comprehensive multilateral international sanctions on Iraq and freezing all its foreign assets. Iraq was no longer free to import anything not expressly permitted by the United Nations, and companies were forbidden from doing business with Iraq, with very limited exceptions. Before the conflict started, Iraq had imported roughly 70 percent of its food, medicine, and chemicals for agriculture. Although its oil reserves, and hence its wealth, were virtually limitless, it was nonetheless a country that without international trade could not feed itself or sustain the modern developed society it was becoming.

On February 28, 1991, Iraq, defeated on the battlefield, capitulated to American-led forces. The sanctions remained in place. On August 27, 1992, the United Nations declared "no fly" zones over the Shiite areas of southern Iraq and the Kurdish areas of the country's north, adding physical containment of Hussein's military to the program of sanctions. This created a policy that several Clinton administration officials would later describe to me as "keeping Saddam in his box."

By early 1993, opposition to sanctions was growing, especially in the Arab world, and so was dissension within the United Nations. Albright, then Washington's newly appointed ambassador to the United Nations, recalls that when she arrived in New York to take up her post in February 1993, there was confusion about sanctions policy. As she put it, "No one had thought they would be in place for so long, but then, no one had really thought Saddam Hussein would still be there either. The intelligence was that he'd be gone fairly soon."

Albright's instructions from the White House were to hold "very firm" on sanctions. But she soon made a trip to the Middle East that, while it had been undertaken largely to persuade Middle Eastern leaders that they should support a continuation of sanctions policy, also caused her to somewhat modify her view about what the effects of sanctions were on the ground in Iraq.

"I went to various Arab capitals with photographs we'd declassified that showed how much money Saddam Hussein was spending on his palaces," she told me recently. "The Arab leaders were amazed. They hadn't known any of this. But in turn they told me about how much the Iraqi people were suffering under sanctions. They also talked about the anger over sanctions that was building in the Arab 'street.' Of course, this protest was affecting them, too. But I was appalled by what they told me, not just worried about the political consequences. And it was when I returned to the UN that I began to try to mitigate the humanitarian consequences of the sanctions. That's when the idea of 'food for oil' was born."

The premise of the Oil-for-Food Program, which was administered by the United Nations, was that Saddam Hussein would be allowed to sell a certain amount of oil. With the proceeds, Hussein's government would be permitted to buy essential humanitarian supplies, including food, medicine, and materials needed to keep Iraq's crumbling infrastructure running. A humanitarian coordinator would oversee things in the country, making sure that the materials being imported were used for their stated purposes. The program sought to bar the Iraqi government from obtaining any materials that could be used for military purposes, and as Albright points out, that was problematic: items like chlorine or chemical fertilizer can be used to make poison gas or explosives even if their ostensible use is in water purification or agriculture. "Even shoes can be considered 'dual use' items," Albright told me, "since it all depends on whether they are going to the general population or to the military."

In New York, decisions on what Iraq would be permitted to import and what it would be barred from obtaining were made in a special United Nations sanctions body, the so-called 661 Committee, named after the Security Council resolution that had imposed sanctions in the first place. Outside the United Nations, pressure to do something to ease the plight of the Iraqi people was mounting. As David M. Malone, a former Canadian ambassador to the United Nations who now runs the International Peace Academy, recalls it, the modifications to the system of Iraq sanctions were the result of "huge publicity and international pressure." First Halliday and then his successor, Hans von Sponeck, resigned the post of United Nations humanitarian coordinator for Iraq in order to protest the sanctions.

But although the Security Council agreed to the Oil-for-Food Program in April 1995, Saddam Hussein at first refused to participate, holding out for a total lifting of sanctions. It seems to have been during this period, when Hussein was trying to wait out the United Nations and the Americans and the British were trying to bring the Baghdad regime to its knees through sanctions, that the worst human suffering in Iraq took place. It was only in December 1996 that Hussein accepted the Oil-for-Food Program, and only in 1997 that it became effective in alleviating some, though not all, of the torments of the Iraqi people.

At the same time, the French and the Russians were pushing hard within the Security Council either for a ratcheting down or an outright lifting of sanctions. Nancy Soderberg states flatly that the French and the Russians allowed their eagerness to develop business deals with Iraq to affect their work on the 661 Committee. "The French and Russians wanted to make money," she told me. "By the time of the Second Gulf War, the Russians had $40 billion in prospective deals with Saddam Hussein's regime." (As for the French, as the International Peace Academy's David Malone puts it, "Paris never offered an effective alternative to sanctions, simply grandstanding on humanitarian questions while doing business with Iraq.")

Meanwhile, at the General Assembly, governments of a majority of the countries in the developing world were actively denouncing sanctions as wantonly brutal—as a policy that in effect punished the Iraqi people in the cruelest possible manner without weakening Saddam Hussein's grip on power in the slightest.

In Washington, there was a growing sense that sanctions were a trap from which the United States was unable to extricate itself. Lee Feinstein, who was a senior State Department official during the Clinton administration and who was involved with Iraq policy, told me somewhat despairingly that the decision to continue with sanctions was as much as anything the result of there having been no other options that were politically feasible.

"We had a hostile Congress that would have leapt down our throats had we drastically loosened the sanctions," he said. "We had the French at the UN pushing for an outright lifting of sanctions. And we had Saddam Hussein, who was a real threat."

That is the way sanctions looked from the United States and Europe. But it was difficult, during the debate in the 1990s, to know what the Iraqi people really thought. This is no longer true. The Iraq I traveled to in May was full of dissonant voices and contradictory opinions. People were no longer afraid to speak their minds. And yet what I found was an almost universal opposition to sanctions—a stern, unshakable conviction that the 1990s were a human and economic catastrophe for the Iraqi people and that sanctions were at the heart of the disaster.

Khaled Afra, a young physics student I met shortly after I arrived in Baghdad, phrased it this way: "Saddam was a criminal, the biggest. But sanctions were also criminal. There was a huge amount of victims due to illness. You see, sanctions really killed our dreams—not my personal dreams only, but those of my Iraqi people, all of us."

You can still see the effects of sanctions everywhere in Baghdad. It's not only in the degradation of the infrastructure of daily life; it's also in the remnants of the food-rationing program that Hussein's government instituted to deal with sanctions.

In every neighborhood of every Iraqi city and town, there are a number of small stores, approximately one for every fifty or sixty families, that warehoused the monthly government ration of food staples on which most Iraqis depended for their physical survival. Essential items like flour, sugar, rice, cooking oil, lentils, and beans were distributed to these "agencies"—the term English-speaking Iraqis customarily use to describe them—by Saddam Hussein's Ministry of Trade. (The stores are still in use today because the American occupation authorities have not been able to devise a better way to get cheap food staples to the general population.) The shops tend to be small and, even by the standards of a place that is as decayed and dilapidated as contemporary Iraq, far shabbier than the shops that surround them. They are the front line of what sanctions actually wrought in Iraq.

"I do not make money from selling these things to my neighbors," a merchant named Salman Moussa told me as we stood in front of his agency in the Baghdad neighborhood of Al Mansour. "Basically, I am doing a public service." After a long pause, he finally added, "Like a fireman. Since the prices are so low—a few American dollars each month for all the food—merchants like me only make a little profit."

Most Iraqis and most outside observers agree that food was the area in which Saddam Hussein's government coped best with sanctions. Kenny Gluck, a seasoned American relief worker who is now the operations director for the Dutch section of Doctors Without Borders, remarked to me recently, "You can't say too many bad things about Saddam Hussein, but give the devil his due: on the food issue, he responded very capably."

The food success buttresses the case of those who always claimed that the toll exacted on the Iraqi people through sanctions was all the fault of Saddam Hussein. He could have provided Iraqis what they needed all along, they say. But instead of doing so, he chose to devote his country's resources to building palaces for himself and for his family and functionaries, mosques to please the disaffected believers among his citizens and weapons with which to menace his neighbors and the world. To a limited extent, anyway, many Iraqis seem to agree with this analysis.

"Saddam could do many things to the people," a former Iraqi

Army officer named Raed Mohammed told me, "but while he could kill them, he could not afford to starve them. So yes, he made sure the Ministry of Trade organized things correctly. As a result, the rationing was popular. It helped the regime maintain its legitimacy. Most people thought, 'Saddam is feeding us while the Americans are trying to starve us to death.'"

Indeed, Hussein's government was so proud of its accomplishment that in front of the Ministry of Trade headquarters, there was a huge mural of Saddam Hussein showing the tyrant holding up a ration book—his "gift" to the Iraqi people. (The mural was later defaced by looters.) And there were other, unanticipated, advantages that accrued to the regime from the rationing system. Every Iraqi head of household had to have such a ration book, issued by the Ministry of Trade, which named every immediate family member and listed the precise quantities of foodstuffs to which the bearer was entitled. Every food agent had a computerized list from the Ministry of Trade of the people he was supposed to supply with these staples.

What this meant in practice was that the regime could maintain a database on every Iraqi citizen and constantly update it, without recourse to the security services or even a network of paid informants. It was a secret policeman's dream—and it was all provided, however inadvertently, by the sanctions the United States and Britain had conceived as a way of limiting Saddam Hussein's power.

"First we got used to the idea that the government provided food," a young Iraqi journalism student named Aziz told me. (He preferred that I not know his last name.) "Then we started to see the government as the provider of absolutely everything. For Saddam, it was great. The more he controlled distribution, the more effective the Iraqi police state became. After all, practically the worst thing you could do was to lose your ration card."

In many ways, Saddam Hussein became a master at manipulating the sanctions system to his own ends. Under the rubric of the Oil-for-Food Program, the United Nations allowed the Iraqis themselves to publish their list of humanitarian requirements and then to select the foreign companies with which they wished to do business. This provision meant that the Iraqi government was able to set up a well-orchestrated system of kickback schemes in which a contract would be signed at far more than the cost of fulfilling it, with the difference deposited secretly by the selected contractors in Iraqi government-controlled accounts all over the world. As a result, Saddam Hussein and the Baath elite got rich off the sanctions, and a great many international businessmen, notably in the Arab world, in France, and in Russia, made handsome profits as well.

"The Syrians, the Jordanians, the Turks—they all had their own deals," Nancy Soderberg recalls.

Meanwhile, Saddam Hussein used the pretext of the sanctions to wage a propaganda war—one that even many American officials would later concede he probably won. Not only did Hussein use the sanctions to rationalize to Iraqis every shortage they were enduring, but he also proved himself a kind of genius at exaggerating and exploiting the effects of sanctions that were already tragic enough when reported truthfully. To rally his population, and probably also in a bid to win support from Western sympathizers and the international media, Saddam Hussein orchestrated a kind of traffic in suffering—all meant for the television cameras.

One doctor I spoke to who spent several years in a hospital in the provincial city of Baquba, about twenty-five miles north of Baghdad, told me that the hospital staff had instructions, whenever a child died, to keep the corpse in the morgue rather than burying it immediately as mandated by Islamic custom. "When a sufficient number of bodies accumulated," he explained, "the authorities would stage a mass funeral, railing against the sanctions, even though as often as not there was no connection between a particular child's death and the sanctions."

I asked the doctor how a child's parents could possibly have agreed to such a deception.

"This was not a country in which one disagreed," he replied. "And in any case, they got fifty kilos of rice and fifty kilos of flour. Or else they were paid, you know, like the families of the freedom fighters in Palestine."

I inquired whether there had been other manipulations of the system to make things seem worse than they had really been.

"Of course," he replied, as if it were the most obvious thing in the world. "It happened all the time. For example, we would get a shipment from the Ministry of Health of vaccines provided by the World Health Organization. But then we would be instructed not to use them until they had reached or even exceeded their sell-by date. Then the television cameras would come, and we would be told to lie and tell the public how the UN made ordinary Iraqis suffer. You have to understand: This was a system where everyone knew what was expected of them. Most of the time, we didn't even have to be told what to do."

This media campaign was extremely effective. If anything, it was more influential in the West, mobilizing public opinion against sanctions, than it was within Iraq. What began as a campaign of left-wing fringe activists, like Ramsey Clark and the British member of Parliament George Galloway, soon became the dominant opinion. In the late 1990s, United Nations Secretary-General Kofi Annan was privately emphasizing to American and British officials his own moral qualms about the humanitarian effects of Iraq sanctions. As another senior Clinton administration official put it to me, "I still think sanctions were the right policy. But there is no question that in terms of public opinion, as the '90s wore on we were increasingly on the defensive in the sanctions debate."

In Iraq itself, the experience of the doctor in Baquba was anything but unique. Dr. Mohammed al-Alwan, the head of the department of surgery at Baghdad's leading teaching hospital and one of the most prominent physicians in Iraq, told me very much the same thing. "Yes," he said, "the sanctions played a great role in the destruction of our health services and in health care generally. The shortages were extraordinary, particularly with regard to cancer patients, but even descending to such ordinary items as urinary catheters and chest tubes. I don't know what you Americans intended by these sanctions, but I do know that catastrophic effects were intended by Saddam Hussein's regime. The government wanted to say, 'Look, the Iraqi people are suffering so terribly.' But in reality, there were more than enough drugs for 'special' people."

As al-Alwan saw it, Iraq had been subjected to two sets of sanctions, those of the United Nations and those of Saddam Hussein himself. Voices outside Iraq echoed this perspective. Hans von Sponeck, the United Nations coordinator for humanitarian assistance in Iraq who resigned in protest in 2000, remarked bitterly to me in an e-mail message, "Local repression and international sanctions became brothers-in-arms in their quest to punish the Iraqi people for something they had not done."

And the reform of sanctions embodied in the oil-for-food process only partly alleviated the Iraqi people's sufferings. Although Saddam Hussein clearly exaggerated the effects of the sanctions, the 661 Committee was so hampered by American worries over Iraqi imports of dual-use materials, as well as by the patent corruption of the process, that it soon became something of a laughingstock—to everyone, that is, except the Iraqi people whose fate was so largely in its hands.

Most Iraqis I met knew all too well that the European, Middle Eastern, and Asian private companies that the United Nations used as contractors to provide Iraqis with medical supplies routinely bought from third- and fourth-tier suppliers in India, Pakistan, and Indonesia. They know how many contractors got rich off Iraq's predicament. In pharmacies all over the towns and cities of Iraq, it is commonplace to see medicines stamped with the World Health Organization logo along with the phrase "Not for Commercial Sale." These drugs were intended for hospitals. Instead, they were routinely sold to private pharmacists by the Ministry of Health, which was startlingly corrupt even by the standards of Saddam Hussein's Iraq.

In the highly regulated market that sanctions engendered, only the state was in a position to make traders rich by circumventing sanctions or by using them in ways their architects had never intended.

"Everyone traded here," the scion of an important Arab business family told me, asking that I conceal his identity. "Gulfis, Saudis, Egyptians, Russians, Chinese—they all made money out of Iraq and out of sanctions. The poor UN didn't have a clue about what was going on. They were just idiots. It was a bazaar. Every contract was marked up by 10 percent. But Saddam controlled it all, and until the war started, he, not the Americans, was the big winner."

He hardly needed to add who the big loser had been.

The reality of sanctions is very likely the one adduced by Lee Feinstein of the Clinton-era State Department. For implicit in his description of why the Clinton administration acted as it did is the sense that sanctions were less a policy than a stopgap—one that was a tragedy for the Iraqi people but that also turned into a trap for the United States. Soderberg says that the controversy over sanctions allowed Saddam Hussein to transform the debate from one about his compliance with United Nations resolutions to one about the lifting of the sanctions. As a means of containing Hussein, she says, sanctions were successful, but they were a "deteriorating" policy.

And yet as new rogue states emerge and new international crises flare up, the appeal of sanctions remains. They are relatively cheap and virtually cost-free for those who impose them—though they can be terribly costly for those upon whom they are imposed. Symbolically, they can be highly resonant and emotive. "See, we're doing something about Saddam, or Fidel, or Kim Jong Il," policy makers can say to the public and to themselves. The problem is that there is little or no evidence that sanctions do real damage to regimes that are willing to allow their people to suffer and die. In his mad dotage, despite the fact that he is rapturously out of touch with the thinking of ordinary Cubans, Fidel Castro is as strong as ever. The same was true of Saddam Hussein, who was firmly in control in Iraq when the Second Gulf War began; sanctions palpably failed to dislodge his government and in fact strengthened him politically.

One may disagree with the policies the present administration has followed with regard to Iraq—policies that have led to a brilliantly successful war and a staggeringly inept postwar occupation. But to its credit, at least it had a policy, one partly based on the understanding that Iraq sanctions may have contained Hussein, but they had failed at weakening his grip on his country. Brent Scowcroft is right that without the sanctions the American victory in the Second Gulf War might very well not have been as smooth. The embargo does seem to have achieved the goal subsequently advanced for it as a rationale; that is, to keep Hussein "in his box" and to prevent him from developing weapons of mass destruction. (Of course, the absence of weapons of mass destruction bolsters the case for sanctions but vitiates the stated case for the war itself.)

And yet had sanctions really succeeded, presumably there would have been no need for the war at all. Not that every Iraqi I met preferred sanctions to war. To the contrary, some even insisted that given the choice between being subjected to open-ended sanctions and the bloody resolution of an American invasion, they would opt for the latter. "I detest the Americans and want them to leave Iraq now, immediately," one Shiite notable told me. "But they got rid of Saddam, and now they have lifted the sanctions. That's good. Otherwise, who knows how long this slow death by water torture, which the sanctions were for us, would have gone on?"

James Rubin, the former State Department spokesman who largely rejects the notion that sanctions had such terrible human costs (at least once the Oil-for-Food Program was up and running), argues that before September 11 turned the parameters of American foreign policy inside out, war was not an option in Iraq. Given that fact, he says, the Clinton administration's choice was between giving Saddam a free hand or trying to limit what he could do through a sanctions regime. Rubin believes that American policy makers faced with rogue regimes have just three basic options—doing nothing, using military force, and imposing sanctions—and so he remains convinced that for all their drawbacks, sanctions will have a future.

"For those who cannot countenance the use of military force, sanctions will always be an option," Rubin says. "Those who believe, as many of America's critics in the world do, that war is no longer a legitimate means in the modern world except in self-defense or with UN Security Council authorization will have to turn to sanctions as the ultimate method of coercion in international relations."

He points to the fact that in the run-up to the Second Gulf War, many of the same countries and campaign groups that had pushed hardest for the lifting of sanctions began to insist that sanctions and containment should be given time to work. "After spending 1995 to 2000 criticizing Iraq sanctions, the Germans and French fell in love with containment," Rubin observes sardonically. "They wanted better, more extensive containment. They were ready to rethink their opposition to sanctions."

We did not see the end of radical evil with the demise of Saddam Hussein. One has only to think of Robert Mugabe, Kim Jong Il or Charles Taylor to recognize that. Sooner or later, powerful states confronted by such a figure are almost certain to turn to sanctions as part of what Albright calls the diplomatic "tool box." In fact, the United States now has sanctions in place against about a dozen countries, including North Korea, Cuba, Zimbabwe, Syria, and Libya. Just this month, Congress imposed a new array of economic sanctions against Myanmar after the military government in that country detained the opposition leader Aung San Suu Kyi.

Some policy makers believe, in my view overly optimistically, that sanctions as now conceived are actually far less destructive and far more sensitively calibrated than they were eight or ten years ago. There is talk now in diplomatic circles of "smart sanctions," "targeted sanctions," and carefully balanced combinations of sanctions for noncompliance and rewards for compliance.

And there is always the example of apartheid South Africa—the one instance where comprehensive, multilateral sanctions do appear to have succeeded in producing "regime change." To antisanctions campaigners, however, the South African case is the exception that proves the rule, rather than serving as a model for future confrontations with unsavory regimes. In South Africa, they point out, the humanitarian costs were low (South Africa was nowhere near so dependent on imported staples), and there was an effective and viable opposition in the African National Congress.

Even advocates of sanctions are convinced that the approach that helped bring about the end of apartheid has to be radically rethought for the twenty-first century—and that, they say, is exactly what is happening now. The blunt instrument that was applied to Iraq is in the process of being reformed. "We were learning as we went in Iraq," Nancy Soderberg told me. "We're still learning."

In all likelihood, it will be a costly lesson, for there is this terrible conundrum at the heart of every sanctions policy: while sanctions imply rationality—the knowledge on both sides that the pressure being applied can be lessened by compliance—tyrants like Hussein and Mugabe are often fundamentally irrational. And so my own sense is that sanctions, even the "smartest" sanctions, will continue to exact an appalling human toll.

There may indeed be no way around them. But in that case, we should be clear about what we are really saying, which is that there is no way around the ruined lives and the dead bodies strewn across the ruins of broken societies either. Ultimately, as hard as some officials like Albright tried to mitigate the worst effects of Iraq sanctions through oil-for-food and other reforms, opting for them meant choosing American security over Iraqi mass suffering. If tragedy, as the German philosopher Hegel said, is the conflict of two rights, then sanctions are truly a tragedy.

BLUEPRINT FOR A MESS

On the streets of Baghdad today, Americans do not feel welcome. United States military personnel in the city are hunkered down behind acres of fencing and razor wire inside what was once Saddam Hussein's Republican Palace. When L. Paul Bremer III, head of the Coalition Provisional Authority, leaves the compound, he is always surrounded by bodyguards, carbines at the ready, and GIs on patrol in the city's streets never let their hands stray far from the triggers of their machine guns or M-16 rifles. The official line from the White House and the Pentagon is that things in Baghdad and throughout Iraq are improving. But an average of thirty-five attacks are mounted each day on American forces inside Iraq by armed resisters of one kind or another, whom American commanders concede are operating with greater and greater sophistication. In the back streets of Sadr City, the impoverished Baghdad suburb where almost two million Shiites live—and where Bush administration officials and Iraqi exiles once imagined American troops would be welcomed with sweets and flowers—the mood, when I visited in September, was angry and resentful. In October, the twenty-four-member American-appointed Iraqi Governing Council warned of a deteriorating security situation.

Historically, it is rare that a warm welcome is extended to an occupying military force for very long, unless, that is, the postwar goes very smoothly. And in Iraq, the postwar occupation has not gone smoothly.

I HAVE MADE two trips to Iraq since the end of the war and interviewed dozens of sources in Iraq and in the United States who were involved in the planning and execution of the war and its aftermath. It is becoming painfully clear that the American plan (if it can even be dignified with the name) for dealing with postwar Iraq was flawed in its conception and ineptly carried out. At the very least, the bulk of the evidence suggests that what was probably bound to be a difficult aftermath to the war was made far more difficult by blinkered vision and overoptimistic assumptions on the part of the war's greatest partisans within the Bush administration. The lack of security and order on the ground in Iraq today is in large measure a result of decisions made and not made in Washington before the war started, and of the specific approaches toward coping with postwar Iraq undertaken by American civilian officials and military commanders in the immediate aftermath of the war.

Despite administration claims, it is simply not true that no one could have predicted the chaos that ensued after the fall of Saddam Hussein. In fact, many officials in the United States, both military and civilian, as well as many Iraqi exiles, predicted quite accurately the perilous state of things that exists in Iraq today. There was ample warning, both on the basis of the specifics of Iraq and the precedent of other postwar deployments—in Panama, Kosovo, and elsewhere—that the situation in postwar Iraq was going to be difficult and might become unmanageable. What went wrong was not that no one could know or that no one spoke out. What went wrong is that the voices of Iraq experts, of the State Department almost in its entirety, and, indeed, of important segments of the uniformed military were ignored. As much as the invasion of Iraq and the rout of Saddam Hussein and his army was a triumph of planning and implementation, the mess that is postwar Iraq is a failure of planning and implementation.

GETTING IN TOO DEEP WITH CHALABI

IN THE MINDS of the top officials of the Department of Defense during the run-up to the war, Iraq by the end of this year would have enough oil flowing to help pay for the country's reconstruction, a constitution nearly written and set for ratification and, perhaps most important, a popular new leader who shared America's vision not only for Iraq's future but also for the Middle East's.

Ahmad Chalabi may on the face of it seem an odd figure to count on to unify and lead a fractious postwar nation that had endured decades of tyrannical rule. His background is in mathematics and banking, he is a secular Shiite Muslim and he had not been in Baghdad since the late 1950s. But in the early 1990s he became close to Richard Perle, who was an assistant secretary of defense in the Reagan administration, and in 1992, in the wake of the first gulf war, he founded the Iraqi National Congress, an umbrella organization of Iraqi opposition groups in exile.

In the mid-1990s, Chalabi attended conferences on a post-Hussein Iraq organized by Perle and sponsored by the American

Enterprise Institute. There he met a group of neoconservative and conservative intellectuals who had served in the administrations of Ronald Reagan and George H.W. Bush, including Dick Cheney, Donald Rumsfeld, and Paul Wolfowitz, who later formed the core group that would persuade President George W. Bush to go to war with Iraq. As a number of Iraqi exiles have since related, Wolfowitz, then the dean of the Nitze School of Advanced International Studies at Johns Hopkins University, was particularly appalled and shamed by the first Bush administration's failure to help the Kurds and the southern Shiites in the aftermath of the First Gulf War. Encouraged by President Bush to "take matters into their own hands," these groups had risen against Saddam Hussein, only to be crushed by his forces while America did nothing. Wolfowitz and his colleagues believed that removing Saddam Hussein would have been the right way to end the First Gulf War, and during their years out of power they lobbied the Clinton administration both publicly and privately to make the overthrow of Saddam Hussein a priority.

Later in the decade, Chalabi fell out of favor with the CIA and the State Department, which questioned his popular support in Iraq and accused him of misappropriating American government funds earmarked for armed resistance by Iraqi exile groups against Saddam Hussein. He remained close with Perle and Wolfowitz, however, as well as with other neoconservative figures in Washington, including Douglas Feith, a former aide to Perle, and regularly appeared with them on panels at conservative policy institutes like the Heritage Foundation and the American Enterprise Institute. Chalabi lobbied senators and congressmen to support action against Saddam Hussein, and a coalition of neoconservatives, including Rumsfeld, Wolfowitz, and Perle, sent a letter to President Clinton calling for a tougher Iraq policy. Together they succeeded in persuading the Republican-controlled Congress in 1998 to pass the Iraq Liberation Act, signed into law by President Clinton, a piece of legislation that made regime change in Iraq the official policy of the United States.

After George W. Bush assumed the presidency, Chalabi's Washington allies were appointed to senior positions in the defense establishment. Wolfowitz became deputy defense secretary, Feith under secretary of defense for policy and Perle head of the Defense Policy Board. Chalabi and the neoconservatives in the Pentagon were united by a shared vision of a radically reshaped Middle East and a belief that the overthrow of Saddam Hussein was the essential first step in the realization of that vision. The Iraq Chalabi envisioned—one that would make peace with Israel, have adversarial relations with Iran, and become a democratic model for (or, seen another way, a threat to) Saudi Arabia—coincided neatly with the plan of the administration neoconservatives, who saw post-Hussein Iraq as a launching pad for what they described as the democratization of the Middle East. (Wolfowitz, Perle, and Chalabi all refused or did not respond to requests to be interviewed for this article.)

Bush had come into office strenuously opposing "nation building," and in the early months of his presidency the neoconservatives' interventionist view was by no means dominant. But the attacks of September 11, 2001, gave the movement new energy. Within days of the attacks, Wolfowitz was spearheading efforts to put on the table a plan to overthrow Saddam Hussein.

Initially these efforts seemed to go nowhere. There was the war in Afghanistan to fight first, and many senior officers within the U.S. armed forces feared that a war in Iraq would stretch

American military capabilities beyond their limit at a time when the threat of war loomed on the Korean Peninsula. But the war in Afghanistan was a quick success, and in early 2002 a vigorous lobbying effort by the neoconservatives, both in public and inside the White House, succeeded in moving the idea of Hussein's overthrow to the center of the administration's foreign policy agenda.

Planning began not only for the war itself but also for its aftermath, and various government departments and agencies initiated projects and study groups to consider the questions of postwar Iraq. As Secretary of Defense Rumsfeld would put it later, planning "began well before there was a decision to go to war. It was extensive."

Chief among these agencies was the so-called Office of Special Plans, set up after the September attacks, reporting to Douglas Feith in the Pentagon. It was given such a vague name, by Feith's own admission, because the administration did not want to have it widely known that there was a special unit in the Pentagon doing its own assessments of intelligence on Iraq. "We didn't think it was wise to create a brand-new office and label it an office of Iraq policy," Feith told the BBC in July.

The office's main purpose was to evaluate the threat of Saddam Hussein's nuclear, chemical, and biological warfare capabilities; its mission reflected the Department of Defense's dissatisfaction with the CIA's conservative estimates of Saddam Hussein's suspected weapons of mass destruction. Chalabi provided the Office of Special Plans with information from defectors ostensibly from Saddam Hussein's weapons programs—defectors who claimed to be able to establish that the Iraqi dictator was actively developing weapons of mass destruction.

Through such efforts, Chalabi grew even closer to those planning the war and what would follow. To these war planners, the Iraqi National Congress became not simply an Iraqi exile group of which Chalabi was a leader, but a kind of government-in-waiting with Chalabi at its head. The Pentagon's plan for postwar Iraq seems to have hinged, until the war itself, on the idea that Chalabi could be dropped into Baghdad and, once there, effect a smooth transition to a new administration.

At the insistence of the civilian administrators in the Pentagon, Chalabi and 500 of his fighters in the Free Iraqi Forces were flown to Nasiriya in southern Iraq in April, in the first weeks of the war. At the time, American military officials were continuing to stress the importance of Chalabi and the Free Iraqi Forces. General Peter Pace, then the vice chairman of the Joint Chiefs of Staff, described them as the "core of the new Iraqi Army." But to the surprise and disappointment of American military leaders on the ground, Chalabi failed to make much of an impression on the people he tried to mobilize.

Timothy Carney, a former American ambassador to Sudan and Haiti who served in the reconstruction team in Iraq just after the war, says that there was, in the Pentagon, "a complete lack of grasp of Chalabi's lack of appeal for ordinary Iraqis." In the end, Chalabi sat out the war in the Iraqi desert and was taken to Baghdad only after the city had fallen and the Americans had moved in.

Many Iraqis outside the Iraqi National Congress felt marginalized by the Pentagon's devotion to Chalabi. According to Isam al-Khafaji, a moderate Iraqi academic who worked with the State Department on prewar planning and later with the American reconstruction office in Baghdad, "What I had originally envisioned—working with allies in a democratic fashion"—soon turned into "collaborating with occupying forces," not what he and other Iraqi exiles had had in mind at all.

Carney agrees. "There was so much reliance on Chalabi in those early days," he says.

SHUTTING OUT STATE

IN THE spring of 2002, as support for a war to oust Saddam Hussein took root within the Bush administration, the State Department began to gather information and draw up its own set of plans for postwar Iraq under the leadership of Thomas Warrick, a longtime State Department official who was then special adviser to the department's Office of Northern Gulf Affairs. This effort involved a great number of Iraqi exiles from across the political spectrum, from monarchists to communists and including the Iraqi National Congress.

Warrick's Future of Iraq Project, as it was called, was an effort to consider almost every question likely to confront a post-Hussein Iraq: the rebuilding of infrastructure, the shape Iraqi democracy might take, the carrying out of transitional justice, and the spurring of economic development. Warrick called on the talents of many of the best Middle Eastern specialists at State and at the CIA. He divided his team into working groups, each of which took on one aspect of the reconstruction.

David L. Phillips, an American conflict-prevention specialist at the Council on Foreign Relations in New York and a former adviser to the State Department, served on the project's "democratic principles" group. In his view of the project, "Iraqis did a lot of important work together looking at the future." But however useful the work itself was, Phillips says, the very process of holding the discussions was even more valuable. "It involved Iraqis coming together, in many cases for the first time, to discuss and try to forge a common vision of Iraq's future," Phillips says.

There were a number of key policy disagreements between State and Defense. The first was over Chalabi. While the Pentagon said that a "government in exile" should be established, presumably led by Chalabi, to be quickly installed in Baghdad following the war, other Iraqis, including the elder statesman of the exile leaders, Adnan Pachachi, insisted that any government installed by United States fiat would be illegitimate in the eyes of the Iraqi people. And the State Department, still convinced that Chalabi had siphoned off money meant for the Iraqi resistance and that he lacked public support, opposed the idea of a shadow government. The State Department managed to win this particular battle, and no government in exile was set up.

There was also a broader disagreement about whether and how quickly Iraq could become a full-fledged democracy. The State Department itself was of two minds on this question. One prewar State Department report, echoing the conventional wisdom among Arabists, asserted that "liberal democracy would be difficult to achieve" in Iraq and that "electoral democracy, were it to emerge, could well be subject to exploitation by anti-American elements." The CIA agreed with this assessment; in March 2003, the agency issued a report that was widely reported to conclude that prospects for democracy in a post-Hussein Iraq were bleak. In contrast, the neoconservatives within the Bush administration, above all within the Department of Defense, consistently asserted that the CIA and the State Department were wrong and that there was no reason to suppose that Iraq could not become a full-fledged democracy, and relatively quickly and smoothly.

But Thomas Warrick, who has refused to be interviewed since the end of the war, was, according to participants in the project, steadfastly committed to Iraqi democracy. Feisal Istrabadi, an Iraqi-American lawyer who also served on the project's democratic principles group, credits Warrick with making the Future of Iraq Project a genuinely democratic and inclusive venture. Warrick, he says, "was fanatically devoted to the idea that no one should be allowed to dominate the Future of Iraq Project and that all voices should be heard—including moderate Islamist voices. It was a remarkable accomplishment."

In fact, Istrabadi rejects the view that the State Department was a holdout against Iraqi democracy. "From Colin Powell on down," he says, "I've spent hundreds of hours with State Department people, and I've never heard one say democracy was not viable in Iraq. Not one."

Although Istrabadi is an admirer of Wolfowitz, he says that the rivalry between State and Defense was so intense that the Future of Iraq Project became anathema to the Pentagon simply because it was a State Department project. "At the Defense Department," he recalls, "we were seen as part of 'them.'" Istrabadi was so disturbed by the fight between Defense and State that on June 1, 2002, he says, he took the matter up personally with Douglas Feith. "I sat with Feith," he recalls, "and said, 'You've got to decide what your policy is.'"

The Future of Iraq Project did draw up detailed reports, which were eventually released to Congress last month and made available to reporters for the *New York Times*. The thirteen volumes, according to the *Times*, warned that "the period immediately after regime change might offer . . . criminals the opportunity to engage in acts of killing, plunder, and looting."

But the Defense Department, which came to oversee postwar planning, would pay little heed to the work of the Future of Iraq Project. General Jay Garner, the retired Army officer who was later given the job of leading the reconstruction of Iraq, says he was instructed by Secretary of Defense Rumsfeld to ignore the Future of Iraq Project.

Garner has said that he asked for Warrick to be added to his staff and that he was turned down by his superiors. Judith Yaphe, a former CIA analyst and a leading expert on Iraqi history, says that Warrick was "blacklisted" by the Pentagon. "He did not support their vision," she told me.

And what was this vision?

Yaphe's answer is unhesitant: "Ahmad Chalabi." But it went further than that: "The Pentagon didn't want to touch anything connected to the Department of State."

None of the senior American officials involved in the Future of Iraq Project were taken on board by the Pentagon's planners. And this loss was considerable. "The Office of Special Plans discarded all of the Future of Iraq Project's planning," David Phillips says. "I don't know why."

To say all this is not to claim that the Future of Iraq Project alone would have prevented the postwar situation from deteriorating as it did. Robert Perito, a former State Department official who is one of the world's leading experts on postconflict police work, says of the Future of Iraq Project: "It was a good idea. It brought the exiles together, a lot of smart people, and its reports were very impressive. But the project never got to the point where things were in place that could be implemented."

Nonetheless, Istrabadi points out that "we in the Future of Iraq Project predicted widespread looting. You didn't have to have a degree from a Boston university to figure that one out. Look at what happened in L.A. after the police failed to act quickly after the Rodney King verdict. It was entirely predictable that in the absence of any authority in Baghdad that you'd have chaos and lawlessness."

According to one participant, Iraqi exiles on the project specifically warned of the dangers of policing postwar Iraq: "Adnan Pachachi's first question to U.S. officials was, 'How would they maintain law and order after the war was over?' They told him not to worry, that things would get back to normal very soon."

TOO LITTLE PLANNING, TOO LATE

The Office of Reconstruction and Humanitarian Assistance (ORHA) was established in the Defense Department, under General Garner's supervision, on January 20, 2003, just eight weeks before the invasion of Iraq. Because the Pentagon had insisted on essentially throwing out the work and the personnel of the Future of Iraq Project, Garner and his planners had to start more or less from scratch. Timothy Carney, who served in ORHA under Garner, explains that ORHA lacked critical personnel once it arrived in Baghdad. "There were scarcely any Arabists [at a senior level] in ORHA in the beginning," Carney says. "Some of us had served in the Arab world, but we were not experts, or fluent Arabic speakers." According to Carney, Defense officials "said that Arabists weren't welcome because they didn't think Iraq could be democratic."

Because of the battle between Defense and State, ORHA, which Douglas Feith called the "U.S. government nerve center" for postwar planning, lacked not only information and personnel but also time. ORHA had only two months to figure out what to plan for, plan for it, and find the people to implement it. A senior Defense official later admitted that in late January "we only had three or four people"; in mid-February, the office conducted a two-day "rehearsal" of the postwar period at the National Defense University in Washington. Judith Yaphe says that "even the Messiah couldn't have organized a program in that short a time."

Although ORHA simply didn't have the time, resources, or expertise in early 2003 to formulate a coherent postwar plan, Feith and others in the Defense Department were telling a different story to Congress. In testimony before the Senate Foreign Relations Committee on February 11, shortly before the beginning of the war, Feith reassured the assembled senators that ORHA was "staffed by officials detailed from departments and agencies throughout the government." Given the freeze-out of the State Department officials from the Future of Iraq Project, this description hardly encompassed the reality of what was actually taking place bureaucratically.

Much of the postwar planning that did get done before the invasion focused on humanitarian efforts—Garner's area of expertise. Through the U.S. Agency for International Development, Washington was planning for a possible humanitarian emergency akin to the one that occurred after the First Gulf War, when hundreds of thousands of Kurds fled their homes in northern Iraq and needed both emergency relief and protection from Saddam Hussein. This operation, led by Garner, had succeeded brilliantly. American planners in 2003 imagined (and planned for) a similar emergency taking place. There were plans drawn up for housing and feeding Iraqi refugees. But there was little thought given to other contingencies—like widespread looting.

Garner told me that while he had expected Iraqis to loot the symbols of the old regime, like Hussein's palaces, he had been utterly unprepared for the systematic looting and destruction of practically every public building in Baghdad. In fairness to Garner, many of the Iraqis I spoke with during my trips were also caught by surprise. One mullah in Sadr City observed to me caustically that he had never seen such wickedness. "People can be weak," he said. "I knew this before, of course, but I did not know how weak. But while I do not say it is the Americans' fault, I simply cannot understand how your soldiers could have stood by and watched. Maybe they are weak, too. Or maybe they are wicked."

One reason for the looting in Baghdad was that there were so many intact buildings to loot. In contrast to their strategy in the First Gulf War, American war planners had been careful not to attack Iraqi infrastructure. This was partly because of their understanding of the laws of war and partly because of their desire to get Iraq back up and running as quickly and smoothly as possible. They seem to have imagined that once Hussein fell, things would go back to normal fairly quickly. But on the ground, the looting and the violence went on and on, and for the most part American forces largely did nothing.

Or rather, they did only one thing—station troops to protect the Iraqi Oil Ministry. This decision to protect only the Oil Ministry—not the National Museum, not the National Library, not the Health Ministry—probably did more than anything else to convince Iraqis uneasy with the occupation that the United States was in Iraq only for the oil. "It is not that they could not protect everything, as they say," a leader in the Hawza, the Shiite religious authority, told me. "It's that they protected nothing else. The Oil Ministry is not off by itself. It's surrounded by other ministries, all of which the Americans allowed to be looted. So what else do you want us to think except that you want our oil?"

As Istrabadi, the Iraqi-American lawyer from the Future of Iraq Project, says, "When the Oil Ministry is the only thing you protect, what do you expect people to think?" And, he adds, "It can't be that U.S. troops didn't know where the National Museum was. All you have to do is follow the signs—they're in English!—to Museum Square."

For its part, the Hawza could do little to protect the seventeen out of twenty-three Iraqi ministries that were gutted by looters, or the National Library, or the National Museum (though sheiks repeatedly called on looters to return the stolen artifacts). But it was the Hawza, and not American forces, that protected many of Baghdad's hospitals from looters—which Hawza leaders never fail to point out when asked whether they would concede that the United States is now doing a great deal of good in Iraq. The memory of this looting is like a bone in Iraq's collective throat and has given rise to conspiracy theories about American motives and actions.

"The U.S. thinks of Iraq as a big cake," one young Iraqi journalist told me. "By letting people loot—and don't tell me they couldn't have stopped the looters if they'd wanted to; look at the war!—they were arranging to get more profits for Mr. Cheney, for Bechtel, for all American corporations."

THE TROOPS: TOO FEW, TOO CONSTRICTED

ON FEBRUARY 25, the Army's chief of staff, General Eric Shinseki, warned Congress that postwar Iraq would require a commitment of "several hundred thousand" U.S. troops. Shinseki's estimate was dismissed out of hand by Rumsfeld, Wolfowitz, and other civilian officials at the Pentagon, where war plans called for a smaller, more agile force than had been used in the First Gulf War. Wolfowitz, for example, told Congress on February 27 that Shinseki's number was "wildly off the mark," adding, "It's hard to conceive that it would take more forces to provide stability in post-Saddam Iraq than it would take to conduct the war itself and secure the surrender of Saddam's security force and his army." Shinseki retired soon afterward.

But Shinseki wasn't the only official who thought there were going to be insufficient troops on the ground to police Iraq in the aftermath of the war. The lack of adequate personnel in the military's plan, especially the military police needed for postconflict work, was pointed out by both senior members of the uniformed military and by seasoned peacekeeping officials in the United Nations secretariat.

Former Ambassador Carney, recalling his first days in Iraq with ORHA, puts it this way, with surprising bitterness: The U.S. military "simply did not understand or give enough priority to the transition from their military mission to our political military mission."

The Department of Defense did not lack for military and civilian officials—men and women who supported the war—counseling in private that policing a country militarily would not be easy. As Robert Perito recalls, "The military was warned there would be looting. There has been major looting in every important postconflict situation of the past decade. The looting in Panama City in the aftermath of the U.S. invasion did more damage to the Panamanian economy than the war itself. And there was vast looting and disorder in Kosovo. We know this."

Securing Iraq militarily after victory on the battlefield was, in the Pentagon's parlance, Phase IV of Operation Iraqi Freedom. Phases I through III were the various stages of the invasion itself; Phase IV involved so-called stability and support operations—in other words, the postwar. The military itself, six months into the occupation, is willing to acknowledge—at least to itself—that it did not plan sufficiently for Phase IV. In its secret report "Operation Iraqi Freedom: Strategic Lessons Learned," a draft of which was obtained by the *Washington Times* in August, the Department of Defense concedes that "late formation of Department of Defense [Phase IV] organizations limited time available for the development of detailed plans and predeployment coordination."

The planning stages of the invasion itself were marked by detailed preparations and frequent rehearsals. Lieutenant Colonel Scott Rutter is a highly decorated U.S. battalion commander whose unit, the Second Battalion, Seventh Infantry of the Third Infantry Division, helped take the Baghdad airport. He says that individual units rehearsed their own roles and the contingencies they might face over and over again. By contrast, the lack of postwar planning made the difficulties the United States faced almost inevitable. "We knew what the tactical end state was supposed to be at the end of the war, but we were never told what the end state, the goal was, for the postwar," Rutter said. (Rutter was on active duty when I spoke to him, but he is scheduled to retire this month.)

Rutter's unit controlled a section of Baghdad in the immediate postwar period, and he was forced to make decisions on his own on everything from how to deal with looters to whether to distribute food. When I asked him in Baghdad in September whether he had rehearsed this or, indeed, whether he received any instructions from up the chain of command, he simply smiled and shook his head.

Rutter's view is confirmed by the After Action report of the Third Infantry Division, a document that is available on an Army Web site but that has received little attention. Running 293 pages and marked "Official Use Only," it is a comprehensive evaluation of the division's performance during the war in Iraq, covering every aspect of operations, from the initial invasion to the postwar period. The tone of the report is mostly self-congratulatory. "Operating considerably beyond existing doctrine," it begins, "the Third Infantry Division (Mechanized) proved that a lethal, flexible and disciplined mechanized force could conduct continuous offensive operations over extended distances for twenty-one days."

If the report contains one preeminent lesson, it is that extensive training is what made the division's success possible. "The roots of the division's successful attack to Baghdad," the authors of the report write, "are found on the training fields of Fort Stewart"—the Third Infantry Division's Georgia base. "A direct correlation can be drawn between the division's training cycle prior to crossing the line of departure and the division's successful attack into Iraq."

But as the report makes clear, no such intensive training was undertaken for postwar operations. As the report's authors note: "Higher headquarters did not provide the Third Infantry Division (Mechanized) with a plan for Phase IV. As a result, Third Infantry Division transitioned into Phase IV in the absence of guidance."

The report concludes that "division planners should have drafted detailed plans on Phase IV operations that would have allowed it"—the Third Infantry Division—"to operate independently outside of guidance from higher headquarters. Critical requirements should have been identified prior to" the beginning of the war, the report states. The division also should have had "a plan to execute" a stability-and-support operation "for at least thirty days."

The report says that such an operation should have included "protecting infrastructure, historic sites, administrative buildings, cultural sites, financial institutions, judicial/legal sites and religious sites." It notes, with hindsight, that "protecting these sites must be planned for early in the planning process." But as the report makes clear, no such planning took place.

Without a plan, without meticulous rehearsal and without orders or, at the very least, guidance from higher up the chain of command, the military is all but paralyzed. And in those crucial first postwar days in Baghdad, American forces (and not only those in the Third Infantry Division) behaved that way, as all around them Baghdad was ransacked and most of the categories of infrastructure named in the report were destroyed or seriously damaged.

Some military analysts go beyond the lack of Phase IV planning and more generally blame the Bush administration's insistence, upon coming into office, that it would no longer commit American armed forces to nation-building missions—a position symbolized by the decision, now being reconsidered, to close the Peacekeeping Institute at the Army War College in Carlisle, Pennsylvania. According to Major General William Nash, now retired from the Army, who commanded U.S. forces in northern Bosnia after the signing of the Dayton peace accords, "This is a democratic army. If the national command authority tells it that it doesn't have to worry about something anymore"—he was talking about peacekeeping—"it stops worrying about it."

It is hardly a secret that within the Army, peacekeeping duty is not the road to career advancement. Civil-affairs officers are not the Army's "high-fliers," Rutter notes.

Nash, understandably proud of his service as commander of U.S. forces in postconflict Bosnia, is chagrined by the way American forces behaved in the immediate aftermath of the fall of Baghdad. "I know they expected to be greeted with flowers and candy," he says, "or at least the civilians in the Pentagon had assured them they would be. But we know from experience that this kind of welcome lasts only a few days at most. You are welcomed with roses—for one day. Then you have to prove yourself, and keep on proving yourself, every succeeding day of the mission. There are no excuses, and few second chances. That was why, when we went into Bosnia, we went in hard. The only way to keep control of the situation, even if people are initially glad to see you, is to take charge immediately and never let go of control. Instead, in postwar Iraq, we just stood around and responded to events, rather than shaping them."

NEGLECTING ORHA

IN HIS Congressional testimony before the war, Douglas Feith described General Garner's mission as head of ORHA as "integrating the work of the three substantive operations" necessary in postwar Iraq. These were humanitarian relief, reconstruction, and civil administration. Garner, Feith said, would ensure that the fledgling ORHA could "plug in smoothly" to the military's command structure on the ground in Iraq. But far from plugging in smoothly to Central Command, ORHA's people found themselves at odds with the military virtually from the start.

Timothy Carney has given the best and most damning account of this dialogue of the deaf between ORHA officials and the U.S. military on the ground in Iraq. "I should have had an inkling of the trouble ahead for our reconstruction team in Iraq," he wrote in a searing op-ed article in the *Washington Post* in late June, "from the hassle we had just trying to get there. About twenty of us from the Organization for Reconstruction and Humanitarian Assistance showed up at a military airport in Kuwait on April 24 for a flight to Baghdad. But some general's plane had broken down, so he had taken ours."

Carney stressed the low priority the military put on ORHA's efforts. "Few in the military understood the urgency of our mission," he wrote, "yet we relied on the military for support. For example, the military commander set rules for transportation: We initially needed a lead military car, followed by the car with civilians and a military vehicle bringing up the rear. But there weren't enough vehicles. One day we had thirty-one scheduled missions and only nine convoys, so twenty-two missions were scrubbed."

More substantively, he added that "no lessons seem to have taken hold from the recent nation-building efforts in Bosnia or Kosovo, so we in ORHA felt as though we were reinventing the wheel." And doing so under virtually impossible constraints. Carney quoted an internal ORHA memorandum arguing that the organization "is not being treated seriously enough by the command given what we are supposed to do."

The lack of respect for the civilian officials in ORHA was a source of astonishment to Lieutenant Colonel Rutter. "I was amazed by what I saw," he says. "There would be a meeting called by Ambassador Bodine"—the official on Garner's staff responsible for Baghdad—"and none of the senior officers would show up. I remember thinking, This isn't right, and also thinking that if it had been a commander who had called the meeting, they would have shown up all right."

Carney attributes some of the blame for ORHA's impotence to the fact that it set up shop in Saddam Hussein's Republican Palace, where "nobody knew where anyone was, and, worse, almost no one really knew what was going on outside the palace. Some of us managed to talk to Iraqis, but not many, since the military didn't want you to go out for security reasons unless accompanied by MPs."

Kevin Henry of CARE, a humanitarian organization active in Iraq, says that he still has similar concerns. "One of my biggest worries," he says, "is the isolation of the palace."

Garner disputes these complaints. He is adamant that he managed to talk with many Iraqis and strongly disagrees with claims that officials in the palace were out of touch. Still, ORHA under Pentagon control was compelled to adhere rigidly to military force–protection rules that were anything but appropriate to the work the civilians at ORHA were trying to do. Larry Hollingworth, a former British colonel and relief specialist who has worked in Sarajevo and Chechnya and who briefly served with ORHA right after Baghdad fell, says that "at the U.S. military's insistence, we traveled out from our fortified headquarters in Saddam's old Republican Palace in armored vehicles, wearing helmets and flak jackets, trying to convince Iraqis that peace was at hand, and that they were safe. It was ridiculous."

And Judith Yaphe adds, "In some ways, we're even more isolated than the British were when they took over Iraq" after World War I.

Kevin Henry has described the Bush administration as peculiarly susceptible to a kind of "liberation theology in which they couldn't get beyond their own rhetoric and see things in Iraq as they really were."

As the spring wore on, administration officials continued to insist publicly that nothing was going seriously wrong in Iraq. But the pressure to do something became too strong to resist. Claiming that it had been a change that had been foreseen all along (though it had not been publicly announced and was news to Garner's staff), President Bush replaced Garner in May with L. Paul Bremer III. Glossing over the fact that Bremer had no experience in postwar reconstruction or nation-building, the Pentagon presented Bremer as a good administrator—something, or so Defense Department officials implied on background, Garner was not.

Bremer's first major act was not auspicious. Garner had resisted the kind of complete deBaathification of Iraqi society that Ahmad Chalabi and some of his allies in Washington had favored. In particular, he had resisted calls to completely disband the Iraqi Army. Instead, he had tried only to fire Baathists and senior military officers against whom real charges of complicity in the regime's crimes could be demonstrated and to use most members of the Iraqi Army as labor battalions for reconstruction projects.

Bremer, however, took the opposite approach. On May 15, he announced the complete disbanding of the Iraqi Army, some 400,000 strong, and the lustration of 50,000 members of the Baath Party. As one U.S. official remarked to me privately, "That was the week we made 450,000 enemies on the ground in Iraq."

The decision—which many sources say was made not by Bremer but in the White House—was disastrous. In a country like Iraq, where the average family size is six, firing 450,000 people amounts to leaving 2,700,000 people without incomes; in other words, more than 10 percent of Iraq's 23 million people. The order produced such bad feeling on the streets of Baghdad that salaries are being reinstated for all soldiers. It is a slow and complicated process, however, and there have been demonstrations by fired military officers in Iraq over the course of the summer and into the fall.

IGNORING THE SHIITES

IT SHOULD have been clear from the start that the success or failure of the American project in postwar Iraq depended not just on the temporary acquiescence of Iraq's Shiite majority but also on its support—or at least its tacit acceptance of a prolonged American presence. Before the war, the Pentagon's planners apparently believed that this would not be a great problem. The Shiite tradition in Iraq, they argued, was nowhere near as radical as it was in neighboring Iran. The planners also seem to have assumed that the overwhelming majority of Iraqi Shiites would welcome American forces as liberators—an assumption based on the fact of the Shiite uprisings in southern Iraq in 1991, in the aftermath of the First Gulf War. American officials do not seem to have taken seriously enough the possibility that the Shiites might welcome their liberation from Saddam Hussein but still view the Americans as unwelcome occupiers who would need to be persuaded, and if necessary compelled, to leave Iraq as soon as possible.

Again, an overestimation of the role of Ahmad Chalabi may

help account for this miscalculation. Chalabi is a Shiite and, based on that fact, the Pentagon's planners initially believed that he would enjoy considerable support from Iraq's Shiite majority. But it rapidly became clear to American commanders on the ground in postwar Iraq that the aristocratic, secular Chalabi enjoyed no huge natural constituency in the country, least of all among the observant Shiite poor.

The Americans gravely underestimated the implications of the intense religious feelings that Iraqi Shiites were suddenly free to manifest after the fall of Saddam Hussein. Making religious freedom possible for the Shiites was one of the great accomplishments of the war, as administration officials rightly claim. But the Shiites soon demonstrated that they were interested in political as well as religious autonomy. And although the Americans provided the latter, their continued presence in Iraq was seen as an obstacle to the former—especially as the occupation dragged on and Secretary Rumsfeld warned of a "long, hard slog ahead."

After the war, American planners thought they might be able to engage with one of the most moderate of the important Shiite ayatollahs, Muhammad Bakr al-Hakim. He was rhetorically anti-American and yet was willing (and urged his followers) to establish a détente with the occupiers. Had he lived, he might have helped the Americans assuage Shiite fears and resentments. But Hakim was assassinated during Friday prayers in the holy city of Najaf on August 29, 2003, along with more than eighty of his followers. At this point, it is not clear who the current American candidate is, although there are reports that American planners now believe they can work with and through Grand Ayatollah Ali al-Sistani.

Meanwhile, in the streets the anger of ordinary Shiites grows hotter. Every reporter who has been in Iraq has encountered it, even if administration officials think they know better. As Robert Perito argues, "One of the things that has saved the U.S. effort is that the Shiites have decided to cooperate with us, however conditionally." But, he adds, "if the Shiites decide that they can't continue to support us, then our position will become untenable."

Although they are, for the most part, not yet ready to rebel, the Shiites' willingness to tolerate the American occupation authorities is growing dangerously thin. "We're happy the Americans got rid of Saddam Hussein," a young member of the Hawza in Sadr City told me. "But we do not approve of replacing 'the tyrant of the age'"—as he referred to Hussein—"with the Americans. We will wait a little longer, but we will fight if things don't change soon."

Or, as his sheik told me later that afternoon at the nearby mosque, so far they "have no orders" from their religious superiors to fight the Americans. Still, he warned, "we have been very nice to them. But the U.S. is not reciprocating." Last month, in the Shiite holy city of Karbala, the first firefights between American forces and Shiite militants took place, suggesting that time may be running out even more quickly than anyone imagined.

THE NEXT STEPS

In Iraq today, there is a steadily increasing disconnect between what the architects of the occupation think they are accomplishing and how Iraqis on the street evaluate postwar progress. And as the security situation fails to improve, these perceptions continue to darken.

The Bush administration fiercely denies that this "alarmist" view accurately reflects Iraqi reality. It insists that the positive account it has been putting forward is the real truth and that the largely downbeat account in much of the press is both inaccurate and unduly despairing. The corner has been turned, administration officials repeat.

Whether the United States is eventually successful in Iraq (and saying the mission "has to succeed," as so many people do in Washington, is not a policy but an expression of faith), even supporters of the current approach of the Coalition Provisional Authority concede that the United States is playing catch-up in Iraq. This is largely, though obviously not entirely, because of the lack of postwar planning during the run-up to the war and the mistakes of the first sixty days after the fall of Saddam Hussein. And the more time passes, the clearer it becomes that what happened in the immediate aftermath of what the administration calls Operation Iraqi Freedom was a self-inflicted wound, a morass of our own making.

Call it liberation or occupation, a dominating American presence in Iraq was probably destined to be more difficult, and more costly in money and in blood, than administration officials claimed in the months leading up to the war. But it need not have been this difficult. Had the military been as meticulous in planning its strategy and tactics for the postwar as it was in planning its actions on the battlefield, the looting of Baghdad, with all its disastrous material and institutional and psychological consequences, might have been stopped before it got out of control. Had the collective knowledge embedded in the Future of Iraq Project been seized upon, rather than repudiated by, the Pentagon after it gained effective control of the war and postwar planning a few months before the war began, a genuine collaboration between the American authorities and Iraqis, both within the country and from the exiles, might have evolved. And had the lessons of nation-building—its practice but also its inevitability in the wars of the twenty-first century—been embraced by the Bush administration, rather than dismissed out of hand, then the opportunities that did exist in postwar Iraq would not have been squandered as, in fact, they were.

The real lesson of the postwar mess is that while occupying and reconstructing Iraq was bound to be difficult, the fact that it may be turning into a quagmire is not a result of fate, but rather (as quagmires usually are) a result of poor planning and wishful thinking. Both have been in evidence to a troubling degree in American policy almost from the moment the decision was made to overthrow Saddam Hussein's bestial dictatorship.

THE SHIITE SURGE

NOT VERY FAR SOUTH OF BAGHDAD, THE SHIITE heartland begins. Unlike the areas north and west of the Iraqi capital—the so-called Sunni Triangle—where there are frequent bombings and the heavy presence of U.S. forces, the Shiite areas of Iraq are relatively quiet. Especially in the shrine cities of Najaf and Karbala, it is rare to see an armored vehicle, and rarer still to hear the rotors of an American helicopter overhead. It is often hard to remember, when you visit, that there was a war at all.

But if the war seems distant, God is everywhere. In the Shiite regions, the images of Saddam Hussein that glowered in various poses from countless walls and ceremonial arches were almost immediately replaced, after the fall of his government, by images of Imam Ali, son-in-law of the Prophet Muhammad, and his son, Imam Hussein. These are the most revered of the first Shiite imams, martyred during the schism in early Islam that divided Muslims into Shiites and Sunnis. Imam Ali was assassinated in a mosque in Kufa, near Najaf, in 661; Imam Hussein was killed in battle near Karbala in 680 in a vain attempt to defeat the Sunni forces he viewed as having usurped his right to the caliphate.

In the markets of Najaf, the Shiite spiritual and academic center, as elsewhere in any heavily Shiite area of Iraq from Baghdad to Basra, you can buy garishly colored posters and cheaply woven rugs with images of Imam Ali and Imam Hussein. Shop windows all over Shiite Iraq are adorned with poster portraits not only of the first Shiite imams but also of more recent martyrs—the Shiite imams murdered during Saddam Hussein's thirty-three-year rule. There are portraits of Ayatollah Muhammad Bakr al-Sadr, a cleric who, along with his sister, was executed in Baghdad in 1980. There are portraits of Ayatollah Muhammad Sadiq al-Sadr, a member of the same family of clerics, who was assassinated in 1999, probably on Saddam Hussein's orders. And there are also portraits of Ayatollah Muhammad Bakr al-Hakim, who returned from exile in Iran after the fall of Saddam Hussein, only to be killed in Najaf last August by a car bomb that also took the lives of more than eighty of his followers.

It is a truism that the past is far more alive in the Arab world than it is in the United States or in Western Europe. This is surely the case in the Shiite areas of Iraq, where the dead sometimes seem to have a greater presence, and certainly more authority, than the living. Talk to Iraqi Shiites, and you can get the disconcerting sense that the conversation—self-evidently to them, incomprehensibly to you—is constantly shifting backward or forward in time. I can't count the number of times, during the weeks I recently spent in the Shiite cities, towns, and neighborhoods of Iraq, that I was told the story of Saddam Hussein murdering Muhammad Sadiq al-Sadr—only to find that in the telling, Sadr's killing became conflated with the murder of Imam Ali more than a millennium earlier.

Iraqi Shiite clerics are quick to acknowledge—some would say exploit—this sense of Shiite victimization, which has existed for much of the modern history of Iraq. The Ottomans, who ruled Iraq before it was Iraq, were Sunnis, and they discriminated against the Shiites almost as a matter of course. When the British arrived in 1915, matters did not change. Six years later, they installed a member of the Sunni Hashemite family brought from outside Iraq as the country's king. When the Baath Party seized power definitively in 1968, it had heavy Shiite support. But once again, Shiite hopes were soon dashed, as Saddam Hussein proved to be even more partisan toward the Sunni, and more violently repressive of the Shiites, than any of his predecessors.

As a result, the Iraqi Shiite political culture is a mixture of grievance and thwarted patriotism. The son of and spokesman for the current ayatollah Hakim summarized the Shiite plaint for me when we spoke in Najaf: "The Iraqi Shiites are the majority here. But they were suffering in previous periods of Iraqi history—since the foundation of the new Iraqi state, in fact. Their rights were never respected. When the Baath Party came to power in 1968, their suffering became a tragedy. We Shiites faced torture, killing, and exclusion from the real life of Iraq. Even religion was repressed."

The Shiites nonetheless remained loyal throughout much of the twentieth century to an Iraqi state that showed little loyalty to them. They led the rebellion against the British in 1920, and, sixty years later, provided most of the manpower in Iraq's war with Iran—a war that Ayatollah Khomeini of Iran wrongly assumed would be won because Iraqi Shiites would not fight fellow Shiites from Iran in defense of a Sunni-dominated regime in Baghdad. Some Shiites finally rose up against Saddam Hussein in 1991, in the aftermath of the Gulf War, convinced they were receiving signals, if not promises, of military support from the Americans who had just driven the Iraqi army out of Kuwait. Instead, American support never materialized, and tens of thousands of Shiites were slaughtered by Hussein's troops.

Once Saddam Hussein was overthrown, it was a foregone conclusion that Sunni dominance of Iraq would end. It soon became clear that the Iraqi Shiite religious leadership had not only survived Hussein's repression with its morale and cohesion intact, but had also quickly established itself as one of the principal forces of order and patronage in post–Baathist Iraq. The failure of American forces to stop the systematic looting in the week after the fall of Baghdad left a vacuum that was filled by hastily improvised militias organized by the Shiite religious council, the Hawza. (It was men from the Hawza who protected Baghdad's hospitals at a time when U.S. commanders were reluctant to commit troops to them.) The failure to quell looting permanently diminished the U.S. in the eyes of ordinary Iraqis; the fact that it was young Shiite men who succeeded in driving the looters away and that Shiite clerics were able to persuade the looters to return what they stole, including works of art from the Iraqi National Museum, increased the prestige of the Shiite leaders among their own people.

American plans for a transition from occupation to Iraqi sovereignty always assumed the approval, or at least the acquiescence, of the Iraqi Shiite religious hierarchy. In the first months after the fall of Hussein, this seemed to be what was taking place. But recent events have proved otherwise. The Shiite clerics have mobilized mass demonstrations against the American plan, serving notice that their wishes can never again be ignored in Iraq.

The Sunni hegemony that began with the Ottoman occupation in the sixteenth century ended with the American occupation at the beginning of the twenty-first century. But there is an unanswered question—the central question facing the U.S. occupation, the United Nations and all Iraqis: What will take its place? Another, more pointed way of putting it is: What do the Shiites ultimately want?

For a nonbeliever, visiting Najaf or Kufa can be a disorienting experience. Near the entry to Najaf, there is a picture of Muhammad Sadiq al-Sadr and the legend, WELCOME TO THE VASTNESS OF ALLEGIANCE. On days of atonement, busloads of young Iraqi men arrive from the surrounding countryside or from Sadr City, the Baghdad suburb three hours north where some two million Shiites live in desperate poverty. The pilgrims come to pray and to listen to their revered imams, and also to flagellate themselves before the great mosques of these towns—something that was forbidden under the old regime. In a sense, they come to show one another, and Iraq, their strength. "We are performing the revolution of Imam Ali," one told me.

For centuries, Najaf and Karbala were among the principal places of pilgrimage for pious Shiites. They were also the places for funerals. Religious injunctions encouraged the faithful to bury their dead in these cities' vast cemeteries. Iraqis call it the "coffin trade," and it has gone on for centuries, to the point that Najaf today really is as much a city of the dead as of the living. Three hundred and sixty-five days a year, there is a constant movement of coffins in and out of the mosques, some accompanied by vast motorcade corteges, others by a few elderly men barely able to carry the casket through the mosque entrance. You see the cars, coffins strapped on top, leaving Shiite neighborhoods of Baghdad for the south, and in Najaf, you see buses taking mourners back to these same Baghdad neighborhoods, the most popular destination being Sadr City.

At every major Shiite shrine, elderly pilgrims—not only Iraqis but now, with Hussein gone, large numbers of Iranians too—are being fleeced by trinket salesmen, as ubiquitous in the Shiite holy cities as they are in Lourdes. Entering one mosque, my interpreter whispered to me, "Watch out for your wallet."

But for all their court-of-miracles aspect, the shrine cities are places of worship, of study, of learned disputation. All the important ayatollahs teach, and there are always supplicants and other clerics present, sipping the tea that is invariably served by some member of the cleric's staff, all waiting for a few words with the sage. Despite the simmering anti-American feeling that pervades the Shiite heartland and the courts of these clerics, the revival of Najaf and Karbala is one of the great accomplishments of the American overthrow of Saddam Hussein.

Even as resolute an anti-American as Moqtadah al-Sadr, the son of the martyred Muhammad Sadiq al-Sadr, admits as much. One morning in late December outside the mosque in Kufa where Sadr preaches, I watched as waves of his militia passed by, beating their breasts and chanting promises to protect Moqtadah with their lives. But even so, during Friday prayers, I heard him admonish his congregants not to forget what a great event Hussein's ouster had been—to celebrate, not mourn, Saddam's recent capture by the Americans. That Sadr felt the need to do so perhaps reveals something about the mood of ordinary Shiites; resentment against the U.S. occupation is by no means restricted to Baghdad and the Sunni Triangle. In Kufa, and also in Karbala and especially in Najaf, the quiet toleration of the occupation seems to be over. With the Baath Party destroyed and Hussein captured, the Shiites are restless for power.

In Saddam Hussein's time, Najaf was a much quieter place.

There were some Iranian pilgrims, to be sure, but relations with Tehran were frozen. And what money the Shiite holy cities earned from pilgrimages was mostly confiscated by the Baathist regime. As a result, even the center of Najaf is far poorer than it should be. There are open sewers near the offices of many of the most important clerics. Thanks to the fall of Hussein, local merchants tell you happily, this will soon change. Yet they mostly revile the American occupation and insist that if called upon to resist it by their ayatollahs, they will do so. "We will be like Imam Hussein fighting the fight for right and justice," one shopkeeper said. "We will martyr ourselves with him as our guide."

Coalition troops keep a very low profile in Najaf. Mostly it is Iraqi police and armed men connected to the mosques who ensure some semblance of order. The mood, however, is not one of uneasiness but of elation. Talk to any Iraqi Shiite on the street, and the sense of relief, vindication and, above all, religious possibility is overwhelming. "Finally I can breathe," one young religious student told me. "We can have our own Shiite imams—real imams, not the official imams Saddam made us listen to."

It would be impertinent to deny the religious aspect of this relief and pride. But there is also a political dimension. For most Shiites there is the very real sense that, as a community, they barely made it through Saddam Hussein's regime intact. In the wake of the failed Shiite uprising of 1991, Hussein turned much of southern Iraq into a Shiite graveyard. Its deserts and its farmlands hold the corpses of the tens of thousands of Shiites murdered by Hussein's security forces. Almost every Iraqi, and certainly every Shiite, seems to believe that the United States encouraged them to rise against Saddam Hussein. The fact that the Americans did nothing to help causes many Shiites to feel great enmity for the

United States. For most Iraqi Shiites, the betrayal of 1991 is a scar that even the overthrow of Saddam Hussein cannot heal.

Moderate voices, including some Iraqi exiles who lobbied hard for the American invasion, will tell you that it was the American decision not simply to liberate Iraq but to declare Iraq an occupied country that has turned the Shiites against the United States. Some radical clerics agree. Moqtadah al-Sadr's deputy in Najaf told me: "The Americans say they're sorry about 1991, and that now they're liberators. At the beginning, in early April, that was very good. But when they declared an occupation, everything changed in our minds.

"Why should we believe the Americans have changed since 1991, when they showed no concern over our fate, when, after tantalizing us, they stood by as we were tortured?" he continued. "It is the same people, Cheney, Bush's son, the Zionist Wolfowitz," he said, referring to Paul Wolfowitz, the deputy defense secretary. "It is not our liberation they want; it is to strengthen Israel and to fight Islam everywhere in the world. We think you are crusaders, not liberators. If you were liberators, you would give us free elections, not the fake ones to put Ahmad Chalabi in power that the Americans want. That is what Moqtadah al-Sadr told Sergio Vieira de Mello"—the UN special representative killed when a truck bomb blew up the UN headquarters in Baghdad last August—"when he came to Najaf. And that is what we believe."

The highest Shiite authority in Iraq is the reclusive Iranian-born grand ayatollah, Ali al-Husseini al-Sistani. It was Sistani, who lives in Najaf, who called for the mass demonstrations of Shiites last month in Basra and Baghdad demanding that the American authorities revoke their plans for indirect Iraqi elections through regional caucuses. Sistani and Moqtadah al-Sadr are considered opponents, rivals for the support of Iraqi Shiites, but in fact the marches represented the views of the entire Shiite religious establishment, radical and conservative alike. The marchers chanted: "No, no to America! Yes, yes to Sistani!" and "Colonialism is not liberty." One of Sistani's honorifics is "marjah," or "the object of emulation"; another chant went, "The object of emulation is the true Iraqi democracy."

When Sistani calls for a direct election, as opposed to the American plan for an indirect voting system based on regional caucuses, what resonates with ordinary Iraqis is their deep skepticism about American motives and their deep resentment of the American occupation. If "one man, one vote" is good enough for the Americans, why isn't it good enough for Iraqis?

The demonstrations in January finally captured Washington's attention, prompting L. Paul Bremer III, administrator of the American-led Coalition Provisional Authority, or CPA, to make an emergency trip to Washington and to the UN. But the truth is that Iraqi Shiites were voicing these concerns almost from the beginning of the occupation. The difference is that until last month, the CPA appears to have believed that it could ignore the wishes of Sistani and his fellow clerics in Najaf. Indeed, in mid-November the CPA and the Iraqi Governing Council signed a deal providing for indirect elections, even though it was clear that Sistani was not going to alter his preference for direct elections.

The Najaf clerics, Sistani in particular, have often been underestimated by outsiders. American observers have compared Sistani to the pope, calling him a man with virtually limitless spiritual authority but little grass-roots organization. Along the same lines, the CPA apparently decided that his assent to their transition plan, while valuable and desirable, would not be essential. Subsequent events have proved this view far too sanguine. The demonstrations have shown that Sistani has enormous support in worldly matters too, as well as the capacity, in a relatively short period of time, to bring his loyalists into the streets.

In a sense, the elections are only the tip of the iceberg. By doing the one thing American officials had feared all along—deploying the Shiite masses in the streets in anti-American protests—Sistani threatens to derail the transition from U.S. occupation to Iraqi sovereignty. The consequences for the future of Iraq, not to mention for the U.S. presidential elections, could be enormous.

The reality driving the fear of a new Shiite mobilization is first and foremost a matter of numbers. While it is impossible to establish a reliable ethnic and sectarian breakdown of the Iraqi population, no one believes that the Shiite proportion is less than 60 percent, and some Shiites put the number higher. Whatever the actual figure, it is large enough to ensure that the views of Iraq's Shiite population can no longer be ignored or put down by force. Soon after the fall of Baghdad last spring, a U.S. official put the matter to me starkly: "If we alienate the Shiites, we've lost the ballgame. The Kurds owe us, and we're the best deal they'll ever see. We can fight the Sunnis. But we can't fight the Shiites, not if they organize against us. There are too many of them."

In the first months of the occupation, Ayatollah Sistani did nothing to actively oppose the presence of the Americans. To the contrary, from the moment the United States and its coalition partners took control of Iraq, the senior Shiite clergy made it clear that it welcomed the overthrow of Saddam Hussein. While not going so far as to urge his followers to welcome the occupation as well—indeed, Sistani has declared that any conversation between an Iraqi and an American should end with the question, "When are you leaving Iraq?"—the grand ayatollah counseled cooperation with U.S. forces, urged his followers to eschew violence and instructed them to bide their time.

This "moderate" view was immediately controversial in some Shiite circles and was opposed outright by radical younger Shiite clerics like Moqtadah al-Sadr, whose power is strongest among the disenfranchised slum population of Baghdad and in Basra and other southern Iraqi cities. Sistani's moderation also enraged both Hussein loyalists and Sunni Islamists, including the Wahhabist guerrillas who have been fighting the Americans in Iraq. As a result, the Shiite establishment has become a frequent target of attacks, the deadliest of which was the massive car bombing in August that killed Ayatollah Muhammad Bakr al-Hakim.

Sistani has little of the charismatic authority of his predecessors, and he was criticized after the war by some Iraqis for having kept a low profile during Saddam Hussein's rule. Cautious under Hussein, Sistani was equally cautious, at first, under the Americans. For that reason, outside observers are somewhat puzzled by Sistani's stiff objection to the U.S. transition plan and his call for Shiites to take to the streets in support of direct elections. "I'm surprised," says Professor Juan Cole of the University of Michigan, a leading scholar of contemporary Iraq. "Once you call for mass demonstrations, you've unleashed something you may not be able to control. Sistani clearly doesn't want turmoil, and yet by doing what he's done, that's precisely what he's risking."

If Sistani decides that he is willing to risk turmoil and calls for further demonstrations, there is little doubt that many Iraqis will follow him. His photograph is ubiquitous in shop windows throughout the Shiite heartland and also in Baghdad's Shiite neighborhoods. In one commercial street in Karrada, a middle-class Baghdad neighborhood, shopkeeper after shopkeeper told me of their devotion to Sistani. "He is our leader," one man said. "We will follow him until our deaths." Another told me, "If the marjah"—the object of emulation— "asks us to fight the Americans, we will do so immediately, happily, to the last drop of our blood." The man spoke with such enthusiasm, I assumed he considered this fight to be both inevitable and imminent. But when I asked him whether he thought the grand ayatollah would in fact call on him to resist the American occupiers, he shook his head emphatically. "Absolutely not," he said. "We Shiites will wait until June"—when the CPA is scheduled to hand over authority for the country to Iraqis. "We will get our country back soon enough."

This ability to wait is often said to accompany the Shiites' almost cultic fascination with martyrdom and suffering. This stereotype, like all stereotypes, is at best a half-truth. But in the fall of 2003, the dominant view in Shiite Iraq was that there was nothing to be gained and much to be lost by confronting the Americans directly. Whatever firebrands like Moqtadah al-Sadr might say, it was better to wait the Americans out.

There are all sorts of explanations for this. One, put to me by Joseph Wilson IV, former U.S. chargé d'affaires in Baghdad, was that as long as Americans were killing Sunnis, the Shiites had no reason not to sit on the sidelines. It was the Sunnis, after all, who had long stood in the way of Shiite rights and Shiite power in Iraq, and by a certain logic, anything that weakened the Sunnis strengthened the Shiites. The Shiites also realize that the Americans are eager to leave as soon as possible—and to leave behind a "democracy" of one kind or another, which cannot help increasing the power of the majority. Having been excluded from power for so long, the Shiite leadership does not want, at the eleventh hour, to ruin its chances of finally acquiring its rightful role in Iraq. "We must wait," one cleric in Najaf told me. And, almost ruefully, he added, "We in the Shiite majority of this country have been waiting to play our rightful role in Iraq since the death of Imam Hussein"—some 1,300 years ago. "Having done that, we can certainly wait another six months."

Not long after talking with that cleric, I met an aide to Ayatollah Bashir al-Najafi, a close associate of Sistani's, and asked him what he thought of that proposition—that the Shiites had been waiting to remake Iraq since the death of Imam Hussein in 680. He grew indignant. "What do you mean, Imam Hussein?" he replied. "We have been waiting since the murder of Imam Ali"—nineteen years before Imam Hussein was killed—"to begin a just Iraq!"

Professor Wamid Nazmi, a distinguished secular Sunni scholar in Baghdad, simply shook his head when I told him the story of the Shiites' 1,300-year-long wait. "Arabs have not yet made their peace with history," he said. "But it is not a question of Sunni or Shiite." On that subject, Nazmi, like many scholarly Iraqis I met, was at pains to insist that the differences between the two sects of Islam should not be exaggerated. "Yes, there are Sunnis and Shiites here," he said wearily, "but they worship the same god, revere the same prophet, read the same holy book." Having said that, he readily conceded that "nowadays in Iraq, the Shiites have become more aware of themselves as a group. Saddam Hussein's opposition to them, his perception during the Iran-Iraq War that they were some sort of fifth column, has made them less accommodating with the Sunnis than they were before."

Nazmi concluded that the Shiite clerics are likely to grow

steadily more powerful. The seeming inevitability of this is what makes the decision of Ayatollah Sistani and his colleagues to order their followers into the streets very difficult to understand. In a certain sense, it seems almost unnecessary. In the summer and fall of 2003, the senior clerics had been firm in their rejection of Moqtadah al-Sadr's demands for an Islamic state led by clerics. As one Iraqi journalist with close links to the Shiite hierarchy in Najaf put it to me in December. "The grand ayatollahs are all opposed to Moqtadah's demands. They think that it is stupid to confront the coalition. And they fear that it will lead to a war among the Shiites—the thing that they fear most in the world." Sistani and his colleagues were able to more or less neutralize Moqtadah—even Moqtadah's own principal aide told me in Najaf that Moqtadah had made "mistakes" that his enemies had "taken advantage of"—and at the end of the year, they seemed to be in a position to influence the course of the future Iraqi state, regardless of the type of election held.

Yet Sistani's call for demonstrations and the rhetoric of those demonstrations were anything but moderate. The crowd shouted slogans like "One man, one vote" and "No, no to appointment," and demonstrators and speakers insisted that they would never accept an American "colonialist" state.

In my experience, American officials, not to mention ordinary American soldiers, reject the idea that they are genuinely disliked in Iraq, except, of course, in the Sunni Triangle. And yet when I spoke to Ayatollah Najafi, his dislike for the United States, like that of most Shiite clerics I met, was palpable. The entry of Sistani and the rest of the Najaf clerical hierarchy into the fray has almost certainly changed the rules of the game in Iraq, not just in terms of the actual decision on what sort of election will be held, but in terms of Iraq's entire post–Saddam Hussein future. Insurgents can harass and kill U.S. forces, but they are doing little to shift power their way in Iraq. With the demonstrations, Sistani managed to fundamentally alter the Iraqi political equation without one of his followers firing a shot. Moqtadah al-Sadr and his followers now have little choice but to fall in line, and Sistani is securing for his Shiite power base greater representation for its interests and its vision of how Iraq should be governed when the nation regains its independence, as early as next summer.

So is this Shiite flexing of political muscle the harbinger of a religious, Shiite-dominated Iraqi state to come? As Ayatollah Najafi put it: "An Islamic state is a wish for us. It will not be achieved until the foreign occupiers stop using Iraqis and stop trying to control Iraqi politics." Moqtadah al-Sadr has been calling for an Islamic state, with the vocal support of his followers in the Shiite slums. And the demonstrators in the streets of Basra last month who cried out that Sistani was Iraqi democracy personified were calling for an Islamic state, too.

But the clerics have not demanded the kind of position in postwar Iraq that their fellow ayatollahs occupy in Iran. The Iraqi Shiite hierarchy has largely rejected, and continues to reject, the Khomeinist view that clerics should rule. Even at the Hawza office in Baghdad, where the political line is closer to Moqtadah al-Sadr than to Sistani, the editor of the Hawza's newspaper told me that "during the 1970s and 1980s, Iraqi Shiites followed the example of Iran. But after the results of the Islamic revolution in Iran and Saddam's humiliation of the Shiites in Iraq, we . . . look at Iran with fear and disappointment. We have to find our own way."

Even if the clerics wanted to emulate Iran, and they don't, Iraq's demographic and historical realities would probably doom any such effort to failure. Although it is true that the Shiites are in the majority, Iraq is not Iran, which is about 90 percent Shiite. The history of Shiism in each country is quite different, as well. Yitzhak Nakash, the author of the definitive *Shi'is of Iraq,* points out that most of Iraq's Shiites are relatively recent converts. In the eighteenth and nineteenth centuries, Iraq—or the areas that the British would, in the 1920s, cobble together into Iraq—was majority Sunni, and Shiism was largely confined to urban areas like Najaf and Karbala. Shiism was at that time viewed as a foreign implant—a charge that Saddam Hussein would later revive and use as his justification for repressing the Shiites and then for his campaign of mass murder against them after the Gulf War.

Because of all this, Shiism simply cannot be the organizing principle of the state in Iraq that it has been in Iran for the past quarter century. And as Nakash points out, it is also the case that the Shiite world seemed, until recently, to have finished its revolutionary phase. "The Shiites, above all in Iraq, have seemed post-revolutionary," Nakash told me. "It is the Sunni world where revolutionary ambitions have real popular or clerical support."

Not everyone in Iraq is convinced that the clerics will stay out of politics. In Baghdad I spoke at length to one of the country's leading secular liberal thinkers, Isam al-Khafaji, a social scientist. While he remains guardedly optimistic about Iraq's future, he says he fears that "unknowingly, we are sliding into the principle of Iranian-style guidance." Few if any of the political parties, he points out, take a position without consulting the Shiite religious authorities. In December, to give but one example, the Iraqi Governing Council voted to rescind longstanding Iraqi civil law. In this scheme, an individual's rights would be administered by clerics from that individual's respective religious community. Thus, a

Shiite woman would have her laws determined by the imam, an Iraqi Christian's by a priest and so on. It is a troubling decree for those desiring a secular democracy in Iraq, made all the more troubling by the fact that women's rights are often cited by the Bush administration as one of its prime commitments in Iraq.

As Khafaji puts it, "When society becomes more conservative, the first victims are women." Obviously, what most Westerners would view as the assault on the rights of women is scarcely restricted to post-Saddam Iraq. Indeed, you see far fewer head scarves among the female students at the University of Baghdad than you do at universities in Jordan or Egypt. Social conservatism is sweeping the Islamic world—above all where the status of women is concerned. Nonetheless, in Iraq there is little doubt that the impetus for these changes comes largely from the Shiite religious authorities.

Wearing a head scarf may be an individual choice, but the prohibition of alcohol, which is taking hold in Iraq, above all in Shiite areas, is not. In Basra, a city now virtually alcohol-free, shadowy Shiite extremist groups like the fifteenth of Shabaan movement, which originated during the Shiite uprising against Saddam Hussein in 1991, have mounted a concerted campaign of terror against Christian liquor-store owners, driving many out of business. Fifteenth of Shabaan and other militant groups have also been accused by Sunni tribal leaders in southern Iraq of trying to drive Sunni property owners from their land. A protest sent to Paul Bremer speaks of "ethnic cleansing" and lists the names of some forty people whom the militants have supposedly expelled or kidnapped.

Baghdad remains an anomaly—a place where, for the moment, anyway, secularism is still alive and well in the schools and streets and nightspots. But in all of the Shiite south and even in Baghdad's Sadr City, a slow-motion Islamization is steadily gathering strength. It is difficult to see how any transitional government, even one shaped by the Iraqi Governing Council and the CPA, could stop this. The fact is that the Shiites are pushing on what may well be an open door. No secular Iraqi party—not the Communists who once led the fight against Saddam Hussein's Baath Party, and not the Iraqi National Congress—seems to be able to garner significant popular support among Iraqis. The Sunnis have yet to deal with what will inevitably be a reduced role in the new Iraq. The Kurds are concerned only with their self-determination, not with taking power nationally. If the Shiites have taken center stage, they have done so by default.

"You can get rid of Saddam Hussein and the Baath Party," says Professor Cole of the University of Michigan. "But you can't get rid of the facts on the ground. And the Shiites are the most important of these facts."

AFTERWORD

DURING THE FIRST YEAR AFTER THE FALL OF Saddam Hussein, U.S. officials both on the ground in Iraq and in Washington repeatedly accused those of us who covered the post-war of focusing only on the bad news and neglecting, as one former senior member of the Coalition Provisional Authority put it in an email to me, "all the good news coming out of the governorates." Perhaps this is why it became commonplace to witness young American soldiers holding journalists at bay while calling out, "Where's Fox News?"

Obviously, it is possible that Iraq will eventually be a decent place to live in, however appalling and degrading a place it is to live in now. And I suppose that for those who agree with American neoconservative orthodoxy and hold that anything is preferable to Saddam Hussein, the bad news from Iraq seems like a transient summer storm—terrifying if you're caught in it but of no great moment if you're not. But to me, the reality of Iraq as I witnessed it from my worm's eye view on the ground in Baghdad and Najaf, always seemed worse than anything I was able to write about it. And as I write this, from Basra to Mosul those "governorates" are in flames. And even if the Sunni insurgents in Fallujah are brought to heel and Moqtadah al-Sadr's Mehdi Army is either broken or co-opted—outcomes that will be terribly costly in blood and suffering—the hatred ordinary Iraqis now bear for American troops and for America seems to me the irreducible legacy of the war, whatever the intentions of those in Washington who conceived the overthrow of Saddam Hussein.

Deputy Defense Secretary Paul Wolfowitz is probably the war's principal architect. And yet even he, after the fact of course, finally was forced to concede that the Bush administration had "overestimated" the willingness of Iraqis to live under U.S. occupation. A weasel word for a fulminant reality. Small wonder, in the presidential campaign, that the administration and its cable TV propagandists were more comfortable talking about a war that ended thirty-one years ago than the war chewing up the lives of young Americans today.

I am not one of those who believes that people like Wolfowitz are inspired by hidden agendas. To the contrary, I am convinced that he is, according to his lights, a believer in democratic revolutions. It is the project itself I have come to doubt. Having once been at least partly of Wolfowitz's party, I find myself increasingly persuaded of the wisdom of John Quincy Adams' Independence Day speech of 1821 in which he insisted—as we know, far too hopefully—that America "knows well that by once enlisting under other banners than her own, were they even the banners of foreign independence, she would involve herself beyond the power of extrication, in all the wars of interest and intrigue, of individual avarice, envy, and ambition, which assume the colors and usurp the standard of freedom. The fundamental maxims of her policy would insensibly change from liberty to force."

That is what I saw on the ground in Iraq, that terrible move from liberty to force of which Adams warned. And in seeing it, I found myself forced to reconsider the assumptions that had undergirded my thinking about force, intervention, and U.S. power for much of the 1990s. For all intents and purposes, I began the decade in Sarajevo, a convinced interventionist. And yet I find myself, at the beginning of the twenty-first century, after the experience of postwar Iraq, convinced that there are very few just wars. To be sure, there are some. But far fewer than either the neoconservatives who seized the policy reins of the Bush administration after the attacks of 9/11 or the human rights activists for whom the United States is both the principal problem of world order and, were its power to be harnessed to humanitarian ends, also the solution to the current disorder seem to believe.

I am willing to concede that, on a certain level, the U.S. invasion of Iraq was conceived of as an act of altruism (its other justifications—weapons of mass destruction, Saddam Hussein's links with Al Qaeda, etc.—have been proved false) by people like Paul Wolfowitz. But what I witnessed on the ground in Iraq was the speed with which altruism can become barbarism. This was particularly relevant to me because, at the time of the Kosovo war, I had written that, if I had to make the choice, I would choose imperialism over barbarism (I have included the essay in which I wrote those words in this collection). In retrospect, though, I did not realize the extent to which imperialism *is* or at least can always become barbarism. Not the only barbarism, to be sure, and unquestionably not the worst. After all, anyone in his or her right mind would certainly rather be subjected to the occupation of the U.S. Marines than Sierra Leone's Revolutionary United Front. But barbarism just the same.

Perhaps Vietnam is not so irrelevant to this debate as many of us would wish. Is not the decision to fight at close quarters in the holiest cemetery in the Shiite world, inevitably desecrating the graves of countless pious people whose great spiritual aspiration was burial in Najaf, the moral equivalent of the U.S. commander's remark in Vietnam that he had to destroy the village in order to save it? Stipulate our good intentions, if you wish. The road to hell still yawns before us. Or at least that is what I have taken back from Iraq.

And I have carried home my doubts about the entire project of humanitarian intervention. Does this mean I am prepared to consistently oppose them? It does not. I still believe we should have sided with the Bosnians and moved heaven and earth to save the Rwandan Tutsis. But it does mean that I am no longer an interventionist, and, in an age where interventionism is the order of the day both on the human rights left (Darfur) and the neoconservative right (Iraq, and now, perhaps, Iran), that means the future seems very bleak indeed . . . and growing bleaker by the day.

ACKNOWLEDGMENTS

IN WHAT HAS BEEN A DIFFICULT YEAR IN MANY ways, I realize that I have been luckier in my professional life than anyone deserves to be. Though I started with neither, I have spent almost my entire career being published by Simon & Schuster and represented by the Wylie Agency. I would never voluntarily leave either. But by now, the people I particularly want to thank, Alice Mayhew and Roger Labrie at S&S and Andrew Wylie, Sarah Chalfant, and Tracy Bohan at Wylie, are far more than colleagues. As friends, though, what I have to say about them is too personal to be aired here. So it is as colleagues, mentors, critics, and dispensers of wise advice and help when it has counted that I thank them, even as I am fully aware that such thanks are scant repayment for what they have done for me. I would not have dared become a writer without Andrew Wylie's relentless faith in my work; I would not have written the books I have written without Alice Mayhew.

A book of essays is a strange beast. Unlike a "normal" book, it is the product of many editorial hands. Here again, I thank my good fortune in having worked with Leon Wieseltier at *The New Republic,* the late James Chace at *The World Policy Journal* when I was its deputy editor, Steve Wasserman at the *Los Angeles Times Book Review,* and, more recently, Monika Bauerlein at *Mother Jones,* David Goodhart and Alex Linklater at *Prospect,* and Enrique Krauze and Julio Trujillo at *Letras Libres.* Those who know them may discern their improving hands in many of these pieces. But the core of this book is my reportage from Iraq, above all the work I have done over the course of the past two years for the *New York Times Magazine.* I have been a freelance writer so long that it has been strange to find a home after all these years. But the *Magazine* has come to seem like home. For that, for their many kindnesses, for their intelligence, and for their friendship, I would like to express my gratitude to the *Magazine*'s editor, Gerry Marzorati, and to my editor, Paul Tough.

Lastly, I want to single out my assistant, Claire Lundberg, without whom this book would never have seen the light of print. I am forever in her debt.

There is an English parlor game in which the players are asked to come up with the phrase they are *least* likely to utter. Once, long ago, I concluded that mine must be: "I don't have an opinion about that." No acknowledgments page is complete without the ritual assumption of blame for all errors and the manumission of friends for blame for all opinions expressed in the work in question. Obviously, I recognize that such a disclaimer is probably unnecessary in my case but I advance it nonetheless, if only for form's sake.

INDEX